Beautiful Lady

Steps to Becoming
a Strong Cancer Warrior

GERI MARONEY

BALBOA.PRESS
A DIVISION OF HAY HOUSE

Balboa Press books may be ordered through booksellers or by contacting:

Balboa Press
A Division of Hay House
1663 Liberty Drive
Bloomington, IN 47403
www.balboapress.com
1 (877) 407-4847

NAB Catholic Serendipity Bible, Copyright 1999 by The Zondervan
Corporation, Grand Rapids, MI 49530 (permission previously received).

Print information available on the last page.

ISBN: 978-1-9822-4843-7 (sc)
ISBN: 978-1-9822-4848-2 (hc)
ISBN: 978-1-9822-4844-4 (e)

Library of Congress Control Number: 2020913330

Balboa Press rev. date: 07/31/2020

ACKNOWLEDGEMENTS

A very special Thank You to Lea Wells who is an incredibly talented artist. I have the privilege of calling Lea as my friend and I am grateful to her for allowing me to use The Beautiful Lady as the cover for my book. This painting speaks to my heart and holds special meaning to me as I journeyed through my battle with breast cancer. Please visit Lea on her website at http://leawellstudio.com/.

Thank you to all my family and friends who walked with me during this battle. Thank you for bringing your notebook to the doctor appointments, being my nursemaid during recovery, taking my late-night phone calls because I can't stop my tears and being my consultant as I completed my new look. Thank you for the hospital visits, the encouraging phone calls and all the kind wishes from family and friends around the world. It was comforting to know prayers were coming from near and far.

No cancer patient can walk this journey alone, and your love and support has been the stable foundation I needed to bounce back.

I dedicate this book to my daughters, Rachel and Jessica.
I am very proud of the women you have become.
Be strong and independent, but lean on others
for love and support.
There is much to be grateful for.

CONTENTS

SECTION 4: SURGERY DAY

SECTION 5: PHYSICAL HEALING

SECTION 6: THE MENTAL AFTERMATH

SECTION 7: MAKING FRIENDS WITH THE ENEMY

SECTION 8: CANCER'S GIFTS

PREFACE

I have a new family.

The support and camaraderie of my new "cancer family" is very strong and is critical to the success of my cancer journey. When diagnosed with cancer, you feel very alone, and it can be very healing to speak to others who know what you are going through. Someone who knows the ups and downs of your particular cancer, the surgery you must endure, and the treatment schedule you are committed to, etc. Every cancer patient needs a cancer-buddy!

When I was diagnosed, I quickly found the forums on websites like https://www.breastcancer.org/. They were a lifesaver to me. I joined a few forums that were most relevant to my situation and introduced myself to the group. Take time to do this for yourself. This isn't a battle you should fight alone. You need the support and these women are angels from God. Do not be shy. You will see what I mean – together we are stronger.

I found women who had just gone through the same surgery I would endure and reading their posts was so comforting to me. Not that they brought sunshine and roses to the picture, because I knew this surgery was going to suck, but that they were honest about how things were going for them. I knew what they considered normal and what challenges I should be aware of, which was both scary and necessary. It allowed me to prepare for what was to come.

Although I have not met any of "my ladies" in person, I feel connected to them and I know that someone on the forum page was always going to post a daily boost of hope or courage, which is something we all need. We need to support one another through this journey. I love my new "cancer family".

Therefore, it is because of the gifts I have received along my journey that I am compelled to write this book and offer you my insights, raw feelings, and gentle hugs for your journey.

I know you feel alone. I know you feel scared. I did too. Some days, I still do. However, please know that you are not alone. Reach out to others every day if you need to. You must stay strong.

"That inner strength, no matter how deep it's buried, is there for you whenever you need it".

Take whatever time you need to feel and release your emotions along this journey. Do not keep things bottled inside. Do not worry about supporting others. During this time, you must support yourself. Feel the fear, sadness and anger and then release these feelings. You need your strength to fight the battle. It is a tough road, but you are a tough warrior and you will get through this.

Although there are many different types of cancer and a wide variety of diagnoses, many steps of this cancer journey are the same regardless of the diagnoses, and I hope that my story can help you feel safe and protected.

I know that it feels like a lonely path, but there are people who will love you through this terrible storm. Your job is to reach out and ask for help from family, friends, and other cancer survivors. Do not walk this path alone. Find a cancer buddy and let's walk together.

I have created this book as a chronicle of my journey and have tried to provide inspirational support through various scripture verses. I have also included questions for own personal journal reflection that should help get you started with your own personal journaling activities. There are no right answers and the questions are there to help you search within yourself to find those areas that need the most healing. Listen to you heart and heal the areas that need healing.

I strongly encourage you to engage in the journaling process. It is so important to your spiritual and emotional healing. Shine a light on the dark places in your heart and take the time to heal them.

Best wishes to you as you walk your cancer journey.

May you find courage, peace and healing, my dear warrior.

Part One

A Storm on the Horizon

CHAPTER 1

A Changed Life?

A s I sit outside on my patio on a beautiful summer morning sipping my morning coffee and enjoying the smells of summer, I am left wondering if today is my last day before breast cancer. I cannot help but wonder if tomorrow's test results will change my life forever.

What if I have breast cancer? How will I manage this terrible news? I am not strong enough for this burden. *Please help me, God. I am more afraid than I have ever been in my life.*

I failed my annual mammogram a few weeks earlier. It had only been a year since my last test, so I was not prepared for the possibility of bad news. They did the first look and asked me to go back to the waiting area so that another nurse could view my results.

Shortly thereafter, I went back for another test and sure enough, Nurse #2 asked me to go back to the waiting area for a second time. "The doctor will be with you shortly", she said. *Ah, no, that is not good. I do not need to see the doctor; I just need you to let me get dressed and get the heck out of here.*

So, I went back and sat in the waiting room. There was a woman there who had watched me come back for the second time and when we made eye contact, I could see concern in her eyes. I was scaring the other ladies who were waiting for their mammograms. Ugh.

I had now been waiting for 20 mins wrapped in this silly hospital gown, cold and getting more concerned by the minute. Finally Nurse #2 came back and led to me a dark room with an ultrasound machine near the table. She told me they had decided to go ahead with the ultrasound today versus scheduling another appointment. She told me the doctor would be in shortly.

Now, nearly an hour after I had entered the office for what was supposed to be a routine mammogram, the doctor finally arrived. She got straight to the point. She told me she was pretty sure it was cancer and that the ultrasound would give her a better look.

Ok. That is not good news. I do not like you, Doctor. I do not like what you just said to me.

Sure enough, the ultrasound confirmed her suspicions and I was immediately booked for the next test called a needle biopsy. She explained that they would "just insert a small needle into the mass and remove some of the tissue." No big deal, it was a simple process.

Well Doctor, I still do not like you. I do not want a needle biopsy.

Fast forward to Needle Day. I did not tell anyone in my family that I had to have this test done because I was too scared to say the words. I thought it was better if I just went alone and got it done.

Holy crap. That hurt like hell. To me it felt more like a tablespoon had been inserted into my boob to pull out "a little tissue." They bandaged me up and I went home to worry. *That totally sucked.*

As I refocus my attention to the beauty of the morning, I find myself making promises to God like If you make the test cancer-free, I promise I will do better. I promise to be a better person. I promise to work harder to serve your will. *Please help me to be cancer-free. I am so anxious and so afraid of what tomorrow might bring.*

Suddenly, I realize that I may have wasted precious time. I think about all the things I have not done yet. I think about all the things I want to do differently. I think about the bucket list I never made and the times I chose work over family.

I promise if you make this test OK, I will be less seriousness, less anger and have more fun. A lot more fun. I promise I will do better, please just make me cancer-free.

Why did I wait for this to happen to make these changes? Why am I one of the thousands of people who say, *I wish I would have done things differently.* I know better. We all know better. We have heard it a million times, "don't wait for something bad to happen to start living your life." But I never thought it would happen to me. *This cannot be happening. I don't deserve this. Please help me.*

Is today really the last day of my life pre-cancer?

God, I hope not.

Healing Inspiration:

Isaiah 40:31
They that hope in the Lord will renew their strength,
They will soar as with eagles' wings;
They will run and not grow weary,
Walk and not grow faint.

Journal Reflections:

1. *How did you feel just before you received the news of your diagnosis?*

2. *What are you most afraid of?*

CHAPTER 2

Ductal What?

Today is a big day.

My doctor told me that my biopsy results would be available today. I woke up scared but excited because I was sure this had all been a big misunderstanding and today, I could finally end this scary storm.

I waited all day for the magic hour when the results were supposed to be ready. Excitedly, I called my doctor's office for the results. Usually it is my doctor's nurse who gives me test results, and the switchboard operator transferred me back to her.

I was holding, and holding, and holding. But, again, it does not go according to plan. When she finally answered the phone, she quickly put me back on hold to look for my file. When she picks up the phone again, I could immediately tell that something is wrong. As she stumbled with her words, I could hear the papers rustling in the background. Then, there was awkward silence and she told me that I needed to speak directly with my doctor, who was unfortunately "unavailable at this time." She said she would have her call me back later in the day.

Wait. What? No way, I have already waited more than half the day, why can't you just tell me the results? I can't wait any longer.

I tried to convince her to give me an indication of the results, but she did not budge. "You need to wait for the doctor to call you back," she said in a very stern voice "I know this is hard for you to hear, but there is nothing more I can tell you. You have to speak to the doctor."

What the hell? What does this mean? Does that mean there is bad news?

This was turning into another scary day.

By the time I hung up the phone I was steaming mad. I was mad that I could not convince the nurse to leak the results, and I was even more mad that the doctor could not step away from whatever she was doing to take my call. I had waited all day. *Fine then, I will wait. I am mad as hell, but I will wait.*

I did not tell anyone that I was having the needle biopsy, so no one knew that today was "results day." I am a single mom, an empty-nester, and I did not want my family to worry.

When I had to go for the needle biopsy, I lied and said the mammogram machine broke for my first mammogram, so I needed to have it redone. I lied because I did not want to prematurely raise any alarms and worry those who love me. In hindsight, I understand now that I lied because I was too terrified to admit the truth. I thought if I did not talk about it, maybe it would go away. I just knew it would come back benign, so it was no big deal. Right?

Right now, I am rethinking my strategy. I have already learned an important lesson in this very early stage of my cancer journey. I should have been open and honest about what was going on with me and I should have told someone how scared I really was.

I already knew I was not going to be able to manage all of this on my own and now, while I waited for the test results, I wished I had shared what was really going on. I now understand why people share the initial news with family and friends-- it is so that there is someone there to help hold you up when the bad news comes.

I was alone. There was no one there to hold me up.

It also occurred to me that I should have told people my scary story so everyone could ask God to take this burden from me or at least ask him to give me the strength I was going to need to get through this.

By this time, I was having quite the pity party. I felt frustrated because this was not fair. I have handled more emotional drama in my life than anyone else I know. *Why does it always feel like*

everything happens to me? Why do I have to deal with this too?!
When is it enough? It was enough a long time ago. *Are you friggin'*
kidding me? Please help me.

Four hours later and I am still waiting for the phone to ring.
My doctor must have been really busy with a lot of other patients,
but didn't she understand, that I needed her to call me? I was
getting more and more anxious by the minute. Ugh.

At 6:01 p.m., I finally decide that the doctor had probably
blown me off for today, so I went to run the errands. I was still very
mad, but I figured it was okay, I would worry about it tomorrow.

Of course, the call came at the most inconvenient time. I was
in the checkout line at Petco when the phone rang; it was the
doctor. I knew I was not in the best position to accept her call,
but I had waited all day and I was not going to miss my chance to
speak to her. So, I was one of the "those" people who would not
get off the phone as the cashier was ringing up my purchase. This
was too important.

My doctor started the conversation by getting straight to the
point. She said, "I have some bad news, but everything is going to
be ok." She started telling me all the details in what sounded like
a foreign language. She was talking so fast.

I remember trying to grasp all the details of what she was
saying while at the same time handing my credit card to the
salesclerk to complete my purchase. He could tell by hearing my
end of the conversation that it was not good news. I had tears
in my eyes and as he handed me my credit card and my bag, he
winked at me and mouthed "I'm sorry". With tears streaming
down my face, I smiled back at him and left the store as quickly
as I could.

I got to my car and started to cry. *I have breast cancer.*

I have Early Stage Ductal Carcinoma, which according to my
doctor, was the good news. She told me that the cancer had not
yet infiltrated, so it was good that we caught it early. She explained
that I would likely need to decide between removing a portion of

the breast tissue along with many weeks of radiation or cutting off my whole boob.

She told me to call her in the morning and she would give me a recommendation for a cancer doctor who could explain the treatment plan to me in greater details. Then, she told me to try not to worry and to get some rest. Conversation over.

I hate today.

Healing Inspiration:

Exodus 15:2-3
My strength and my courage is the Lord,
and he has been my savior.
He is my God. I praise him;
the God of my father, I extol him.
The Lord is a warrior, Lord is his name!

Journal Reflections:

1. *What questions do you have about your diagnosis?*

2. *Write down all your questions and talk to your doctor, you deserve a clear picture.*

CHAPTER 3

I Must Walk this Path Alone

I have always been strong and independent. I admit that I have a higher level of stubbornness than most other people, and I immediately knew how I did not want to be treated during my cancer journey. I did not want to be that "poor lady with cancer." I did not want pity. To save myself and those around me from the future frustration, I decided to make a list of what I did not want people to do:

- *I don't want you to feel sorry for me.* If you feel sorry for me, I will begin to feel sorrow for myself, and that is bad for my recovery. Of course, this is a hard journey, but please try to help me stay positive. Statistics show that an optimistic outlook helps speed the healing process. I am going to need you to stay positive, for my sake.
- *I don't want you to worry.* I can feel when you worry, and it scares me. I can see it in your eyes and hear it in your voice. Just like when you feel sorry for me, if I see and feel your worry, it increases my level of worry. We need to believe that everything is going to be ok. So, please stop worrying.
- *I don't need constant attention.* Please don't think that I am no longer able to be alone. I am going to need a lot of alone time to get myself through this. I love the help and support, but you cannot walk this path for me. I must lead myself out of this dark storm.

After completing my list, it dawned on me, *oh boy, I am such a control freak that I think I even have to tell others how to respond to my diagnosis.*

I have just learned another important lesson. Losing my perceived control is terrifying me more than I ever knew it could. I had plans for my life and getting cancer was definitely not any part of that plan. But I am sorry that I think I am in charge of everything. I'm not in control of anything. I understand that now.

So, I am sorry. Please feel free to support me in whatever way you think is best.

Thank you for your support and I promise to take whatever you want to give me, in whatever form that takes. Thank you.

My Mom always told me that God never gives a person more than they can handle. But I never really bought that story. I felt like I had more challenges in my life than most other people that I knew, and I was mad at God for handing me this burden. To be honest, I was really pissed.

But, one thing I had figured out early in my cancer journey, was that if I had to endure this challenge, there must be lessons that I was meant to learn. A friend shared this saying with me days after my diagnosis. It goes like this, "Sometimes, we need to be hurt in order to grow. We must lose in order to gain. Sometimes, some lessons are learned best through pain."

Today I am terrified, and I do not feel safe, but I am determined to see the lessons I am meant to learn. *Please God, help me stay strong and keep an open heart.*

Healing Inspiration:

Deuteronomy 31:16
Be brave and steadfast; have no fear or dread of them,
for it is the Lord, your God, who marches with you;
he will never fail you or forsake you.

Journal Reflections:

1. *How has your diagnosis made you feel? Are you feeling alone?*

2. *What scares you the most?*

CHAPTER 4

Dear Cancer, You Suck

I am a doer. If there is a problem, I will find a way to solve it. I am also a list maker and I manage projects very well.

When I received my diagnosis, I treated it like a work project that needed a solution with a clear list of tasks to be completed timely and accurately. I spent the first few days calling doctors and assembling my "team". There was so much going on. I needed a cancer doctor and then a plastic surgeon and an oncologist. There were so many people to talk to and so much to learn.

I listened closely to what the experts were telling me, I took good notes, and I organized my decisions carefully.

Because there is cancer in my family and I have one grandmother who had breast cancer and another who had ovarian cancer, I was told I was at a higher risk of developing a more aggressive form of cancer. So, I was especially happy that we found this monster before it had infiltrated to other areas of my body.

Since I have two daughters, my doctor agreed to move forward with the genetic testing to see if I had the BRCA genetic mutations. I spent hours at the doctor's office doing the actual test and answering lots of questions about my family's cancer history. We built a diagram that looked like a family tree that showed who had what cancer. It was scary to look at how many cancer branches there were on that tree.

Waiting for BRCA test results was even more stressful than waiting for the initial biopsy results. *What if my two beautiful daughters were at risk?* That would break my heart.

While I had made great progress toward creating a plan for removing the cancer from my body, I continued to struggle with the emotional turmoil it had laid at my feet. It seemed like adrenaline had carried me through the past few weeks and now that "the plan" was in place, there was more time to consider all sorts of scary outcomes. What would happen next?

Why does everything feel so overwhelming? Why am I so sad? I was lucky to have detected my cancer at an early stage, one that comes with a very high survival rate. So why couldn't I get over my sadness?

I had lost my ability to be strong. I needed my internal strength now more than ever, but my bucket was empty. *Why am I so terrified?* This is a big problem for me – I am afraid that if cancer came once, it could certainly sneak in again, and that terrified me.

I am afraid that I might die.

My logical mind knew that it was crazy things to worry about so many things, but cancer had cracked my foundation. It had put doubt where doubt never existed before. I had never felt this level of emotional terror and it scared me to think that I might have to live in this new space for some time to come.

I am scared and I need someone to help me.

Each day I wake up feeling strong and ready to conquer the challenges of the day, and then out of nowhere, the tears come, and sadness consumes me. My otherwise positive outlook has abandoned me, and I feel betrayed by God.

I am reminded to reach out to others when the path goes dark or when I feel weak. I can't do this alone. I need the strength and support of others. The only way through this storm is straight in front of me. Step by step. Will you shine your light and show me the way?

Healing Inspiration:

Isaiah 41:10
Fear not. I am with you; be not dismayed;
I am your God.
I will strengthen you and help you,
and uphold you with my right hand of justice.

Journal Reflections:

1. *What gives you your greatest strength?*

2. *How can you lean on your friends and family for more support?*

CHAPTER 5

I Don't Trust You

I am sorry, but you must go. I just don't trust you anymore. I am sad to lose you, but I must have boobies I can trust.

I had made my decision. I could not spend the rest of my life worrying if the cancer had come back or if the growth rate had accelerated so that the cancer quickly and quietly had infiltrated to other areas of my body.

Infiltrating. That sounds like such a war-like word. But that is unfortunately the word used to describe breast cancer.

Invasive means that the cancer has "invaded" or spread to the surrounding breast tissues. According to the American Cancer Society, more than 180,000 women in the United States find out they have invasive breast cancer each year. Most of them are diagnosed with invasive ductal carcinoma.

I thank God I have early stage cancer. Thank you, God, my cancer is not infiltrating.

If you read those sentences stand-alone, you might think I had gone crazy. "I thank God I have early stage cancer." What? Although I am very grateful it is early stage, my doctor reminded me time and time again, that cancer is cancer, infiltrating or not, it must go.

I can see why women make aggressive treatment decisions. We cannot live our lives worried of reoccurrence or infiltration. We cannot be continually threatened by a silent enemy.

After much consideration, I decided to take an aggressive approach with my treatment plan and have a double mastectomy. Even after the BRCA test results came back normal, I knew that I could not live with the fear that a lumpectomy would leave.

I need this cancer gone. I need it gone once and for all. I don't ever want to walk this path again. Sorry boobies, but you must go. I will miss you.

Healing Inspiration:

Proverbs 3:56
Trust in the Lord with all your heart,
on your own intelligence, rely not;
In all your ways be mindful of him,
and he will make straight your paths.

Journal Reflections:

1. *How do you struggle with trusting yourself and others?*

2. *Take time for self-care today. What can you do to make yourself feel better? Take a bath or a walk, or both!*

CHAPTER 6

Life Stands Still

I t is nearly three weeks after my diagnosis, and I am still bouncing in and out of denial. I feel fine. I look fine. *I don't feel like I have cancer. I don't look like I have cancer.* Maybe they got it wrong. *Maybe I don't have cancer.* How's that for classic denial?

A fellow breast cancer warrior and dear friend of mine told me it would feel like my world stopped and that everyone else around me just kept going.

She was right.

When you hear the words "you have cancer", there is an almost immediate change in perspective. Things that were muddled and unclear the day before cancer are now much clearer. You now know for sure what is important to you and what is not. The small stuff does not matter, and it is easier than ever before to just let it go. And oddly enough, almost everything is classified as small stuff. It is like someone gave me a new pair of glasses and the view is completely, and forever different

She told me that all those clichés you thought were crazy or annoying, like "take it one day at a time", "don't sweat the small stuff" and "God never gives you more than you can handle" soon become your survival guide. Ugh. I never liked clichés. I have always found them to be oversimplified and annoying. I guess that is about to change.

Aside from the immediate change in perspective, there is also a change in speed. Everything slows down, as if I am in a time warp. I feel like I am in a movie and I just stepped off the train onto the platform and the bullet-train of life keeps whizzing by.

I feel left behind. I feel terrified and I am dreadfully sad.

My once very organized life is not operating as usual. I cannot concentrate because this huge, loud, scary thing called CANCER keeps screaming in my head. I am going to have to modify my life's plan. Modifying the plan was not part of The Plan.

I have cancer. They were not wrong.

Healing Inspiration:

Deuteronomy 30: 8
It is the Lord who marches before you;
he will be with you and will never fail
you or forsake you.
So do not fear or be dismayed.

Journal Reflections:

1. *Are you feeling left behind today, scared, or angry? Write down your feelings and know that you are a strong warrior. You will get through this.*

2. *Reach out to other cancer survivors and ask for support. They can help boost your spirit and help answer your questions.*

CHAPTER 7

This Can't Be Private

I am a very private person who chooses to keep many things to myself. I do not usually share much about my private life, I don't gossip, and I don't spread rumors. I keep to myself and try to follow the teachings of my parents "if you can't say something nice, don't say anything at all."

This is different.

I have realized that cancer cannot be private. I can see now that it takes a village to guide and support anyone fighting a cancer battle. This is not something that can be done alone. Do not even try. The burden is too heavy. I have been in the cancer camp for just a short time and I am already overwhelmed.

On July 14, 2015, me and 4,543 other people across the US received a cancer diagnosis (Per Stand Up to Cancer statistics). An annual mammogram detected my cancer. I did not skip a year. I have done exactly what I was supposed to do. But I still got cancer.

To all my sweet ladies – **do not skip your mammograms**. Go get them done, on time every year. My cancer grew in one year's time, and I cannot imagine if I would have skipped a year or two of mammograms. Things would have likely been so much worse.

Promise you will go. Your life is too important.

I pray that God will bring me strength and courage. Please send positive vibes. This cannot be private.

Healing Inspiration:

Matthew 18: 19-20
Again, I say to you, if two of you agree on earth
about anything for which they are to pray,
it shall be granted to them by my heavenly Father.
For where two or three are gathered together
in my name, there am I in the midst of them.

Journal Reflections:

1. *Have you shared your diagnosis with others? If not, what is stopping you?*

2. *How can your family and friends help bring you courage and strength as you work through your cancer journey?*

Part Two

So Much to Do

CHAPTER 8

Telling my Family

S o, now I knew. I knew I had cancer and I had to tell my family. I knew it would be hard for my girls to accept. We had been through so much in the previous few years and this felt like a cruel blow. I was not sure I was strong enough for the journey, how could I expect them to be strong?

I am so scared, but this must be done.

We were all sitting together watching TV when I began to share the news. There was no way to sugarcoat it and as soon as I said the dreaded words "I have breast cancer", the tears started to flow. They both had panic in their eyes and tears down their face.

I stayed with it and calmly explained the diagnosis. I made sure to highlight the positives; that it was early stage and I would not need chemo, and maybe not radiation.

That calmed their fears a little and they began to ask questions like "When will you have surgery?," "How long will you be in the hospital?," and "Was there a chance I would die?." They had a lot of questions.

We spent a long time walking through the details of my test results, the tests that were yet to come, if they were at risk with the BRCA genes, and if I thought I was going to die. We cried together and talked about all of it. There would be no more secrets.

No, I was not going to die, but it was going to be a long hard road.

Then, they each retreated to their own rooms to process the information in their own individual ways. It was a sad day.

There was no turning back. The news was out.

Healing Inspiration:

Chronicles 28: 20
Then David said to his son Solomon;
"Be firm and steadfast; go work without fear or
discouragement, for the Lord God, my God, is with you.
He will not fail you or abandon you before you have
completed all the work for the service of the house
of the Lord."

Journal Reflections:

1. *What was the hardest part about telling your family about*
    your diagnosis?

2. *How do you feel after having shared your news?*

CHAPTER 9

No, I Don't Want To

Today I am pissed
I am more angry today than I have ever been
I don't want to speak to the surgeon
I don't want to meet the oncologist
I don't want to choose between keeping my boob and losing it
I don't want to spend 35 days getting radiation
I don't want to watch my skin burn
I don't want to tell people
I don't want to have breast cancer
I don't fucking want to

I used to think that losing a boob would not be that big of a deal. It is just a boob, after all. It served its purpose long ago in the breastfeeding of my children, but did I really need it for anything now, right? It is just a boob, right?

Wrong.

It is much bigger and more of an emotional issue than that. I had not considered the psychological impact. It is an emotional decision that is difficult to make.

I am a mess. One minute I think I have made my decision and then the next minute I am taking the whole thing back.

I am single and I am terrified that no one will ever love me again. *Who wants someone with cancer? Who wants someone who got their boobs cut off? Will I have to spend the rest of my life alone?* Ugh. My brain will not stop taunting me with these dreadful thoughts.

How will I decide? They are my boobs and I do not want to make a decision to lose them. *I don't want to decide.*

I feel so sad. I feel so hopeless.

Healing Inspiration:

Psalm 51: 12-14
A clean heart create for me, God;
renew in me a steadfast spirit.
do not drive me from your presence,
nor take from me your holy spirit.
Restore my joy in your salvation;
sustain in me a willing spirit.

Journal Reflections:

1. *How are you dealing with your anger around your diagnosis? Write down your feelings and brainstorm ways to let them go.*

2. *Do something kind for yourself. Go splurge on a nice lunch, or maybe a new handbag. Make yourself happy today.*

CHAPTER 10

One Blow After Another

Today was another bad day. I wonder when the bad news will stop.

Cancer patients should not have to endure financial devastation alongside the devastating health news. On Day One I was told I had cancer, and on Day Four I was told that my employer did not have a standard short-term disability program that I would need while away from work recovering from cancer. What? Doesn't every employer offer Short Term Disability coverage? Ah, no.

Only a few states mandate short-term disability coverage and the level of coverage varies. In my case, it was estimated that I would receive approximately $400 per month. Per month? What? How in the world would I survive? How would I pay my bills?

What am I supposed to do? Cancer will not just "hold on" while I figure out the financial impacts of how to pay my bills. I was being told I needed to move forward with surgery as quickly as possible, but I was stuck with trying to figure out how not to go bankrupt or become homeless while I recovered from cancer.

Our system is screwed up. It is not right that people who are fighting for their lives in a battle against cancer also must fight for basic financial assistance.

I think back to what my friend told me at the beginning of my diagnosis; that I would feel like I had been left behind and that the world was moving along without me. *That is exactly how I am feeling today. I feel like I am screaming, and no one can hear me. Am I invisible?*

What am I supposed to do?

It is terrible that we let this happen. Fighting cancer should be the only thing that a cancer patient has to focus on. Worrying about how to pay the bills and keep the mortgage current should absolutely not be what cancer patients worry about.

This is just wrong. Something must be done.

Healing Inspiration:

Philippians 4: 19-20
My God will fully supply whatever you need,
in accordance with his glorious riches in Christ Jesus.
To our God and Father, glory forever and ever. Amen.

Journal Reflections:

1. *Are you worried about the financial impacts of your diagnosis?*

2. *Share your concerns with your doctor so that he/she can refer you to the appropriate resources for help.*

CHAPTER 11

You are Not Alone

I learned something new today. When you get cancer, you get a Navigator.

It is not a car. A Navigator is a wonderful person assigned to help you maneuver through all the data that you are given when you are newly diagnosed with cancer. Today I was introduced to Lori, my Navigator.

Lori called me and we spent the better part of an hour talking through the next steps of my cancer journey. She explained everything very clearly in real terms - no crazy medical terms; just kind, encouraging words to help me understand.

When I felt overwhelmed, Lori stopped, and we went over the details again. It is like learning a completely new language. Cancer type, level, stage, invasive, non-invasive, infiltrating, hormone receptor assay, ER+, PR+, etc.

It seemed to go on and on, but eventually I could repeat back to her all the details of my diagnosis. I was learning so much about the terrible nuances of breast cancer. This disease causes so much pain and suffering. I felt a collective sadness for all my Pink Sisters who were dealing with their own version of dreadful cancer news.

But I want to thank Lori for her calm, patient, kind heart and for helping me learn this terrible new language. She will be there to help me throughout this dreadful storm.

Thank God for Lori, my Navigator.

Healing Inspiration:

Psalm 86: 5-7
Lord, you are kind and forgiving, most loving
to all who call on you. Lord, hear my prayer;
listen to my cry for help. In this time of trouble
I call, for you will answer me.

Journal Reflections:

1. *What is your biggest challenge today? Write down what is bothering you and how you might take steps to ease your burden.*

2. *How are you feeling about your diagnosis? Are you feeling alone? Fear and abandonment are powerful emotions. Be gentle with yourself today.*

CHAPTER 12

The Confusing Path

There are so many decisions that need to be made within a matter of days of receiving a cancer diagnosis. For me, the first choice was between lumpectomy and mastectomy.

Today was my first visit to meet my cancer doctor. *Ugh. I don't want a cancer doctor.* But I was ready to go. I had prepared a full page of questions and my sister came with me to help take notes.

I liked my new cancer doctor.

She was very kind and patient and sat with us as I went down my list of questions one by one. When she explained the choices, she also shared a variety of statistics about the "success rate" for each option. Lumpectomy was an easier procedure and the statistics of reoccurrence were moderate to low, while mastectomy was a harder surgery but had a lower rate of reoccurrence. I was surprised to learn that a mastectomy did not automatically guarantee a free pass from reoccurrence.

Yeah, lumpectomy sounded easier, but the problem was that my own personal statistics based on experience of friends and family did not align with her published statistics.

Everyone I knew who had chosen the lumpectomy treatment ended up back at the oncologist's office a few years later with a reoccurrence. For those who chose mastectomy, I knew of no reoccurrences. I could not imagine having to endure this nightmare again at any point in the future. Period. I could not imagine having to do this twice.

We talked through my reasoning and she assured me that there was no one clear answer. She said that the choice was personal and that it was entirely up to me. No one would say "good choice/ bad choice," and no one would question my decision.

After much consideration, I decided to take the more aggressive approach and do the mastectomy and while we were at it, and based on my family history, I opted for the double mastectomy.

The decision was made. I was relieved and terrified all at the same time.

Healing Inspiration:

Psalm 57: 2-3
Have mercy on me. God, have mercy on me.
In you I seek shelter.
In the shadow of your wings, I seek shelter
till harm passes by.
I call to God Most High, to God who provides for me.

Journal Reflections:

1. *Has your diagnosis drawn you closer to your faith, or has is created distance for you? Write down how you feel and honor your thoughts.*

2. *Find a quiet place to sit and have a good cry! It's good for your soul.*

CHAPTER 13

The Plan

I am now focused on what will be done, when, and by whom. I am learning so much and have great empathy for my fellow cancer warriors as we fight our way through this terrible battle. I am very sorry for those who must endure the harshest of treatments and wish you strength, peace, and courage.

My cancer is early stage. I feel very lucky. There is 99% chance that I will survive.

My surgery will take place on Sept 15, 2015. It will last fourteen hours and will include a team of two cosmetic surgeons. They will remove skin and fat tissue from my stomach (whoohoo, this is a bit like winning the lottery!) and use it to reconstruct my breasts. It is called DIEP flap. Sounds weird, huh?! The DIEP flap was the most advanced form of breast reconstruction available at the time and it provides a more long-lasting natural outcome over breast implants. I will not have to come back after a period of time to have the breast implants replaced. It is a one-and-done.

That all sounds good, but nothing is ever as simple as it seems. The details of such a surgery are overwhelming.

I am so worried about being under anesthesia for fourteen hours.

That sounds like such a long time. That is nearly two full workdays. How is it possible to be "out" for that long?

What if they can't get me "back?" What if I don't wake up?

Cancer sucks.

Healing Inspiration:

Proverbs 15: 9
In his mind a man plans his course,
but the Lord directs his steps.

Journal Reflections:

1. *Congratulations on making it this far in your journey. Celebrate your success today!*

2. *Name five things that you are most grateful for today and celebrate your gratitude: it a healing emotion during your cancer journey.*

CHAPTER 14

Checking the Cancer Box

I t was time for a break from cancer. Today I went for a massage while vacationing in CA. It had been a tough week and I just wanted an afternoon of relaxation. I was looking forward to a great afternoon.

When I arrived at the spa, I was asked to complete the new client intake form. No big deal, I can do that. The section titled "medical conditions" brought me great anxiety, since there was actually a box titled "Cancer." *What should I do? Should I check the box or skip it?* How could having cancer be a "condition" that a massage therapist would care about?

I quickly scanned the full list. According to their form, I had three medical conditions - cancer, muscle tension, and contacts (which I never really thought of wearing contacts as a condition). I laughed. It seemed like such a silly list.

Still unsure of the relevance, I went ahead and checked the Cancer box.

Soon the receptionist called my name and we went to the massage room. When the therapist saw that I had checked "cancer" all sorts of alarm bells went off, not literally, but figuratively.

It was amazing to watch. She stood there wide-eyed and silent, like she had just been shocked with a jolt of electricity. She was visibly nervous and shuffled the papers around in her hand.

Then she left the room and returned a few minutes later to say they would not be able to proceed with the massage. She did not think it was safe for me to get a massage. What? She said she was afraid to work on me, because she was afraid, she would "spread the cancer." She said she spoke to her manager and they agreed that it was too risky. *What? Was this really happening?*

My relaxing afternoon was quickly slipping away.

She proceeded to tell me that she would only continue with the massage after I called my doctor to get verbal approval. By this time, I was fighting back tears. She sat with me as I fumbled with my phone to call my doctor to seek approval.

As expected, my doctor confirmed that having a massage with cancer was fine and that there was no risk of them spreading the cancer. The news only slightly calmed my massage therapist and it was clear that it was better if I just left the spa. So, I got dressed and left with tears running down my face. *I hate this.*

My first public acknowledgement of cancer did not go very well.

So much for a relaxing afternoon.

Healing Inspiration:

Proverbs 12: 25
Anxiety in a man's heart depresses it,
but a kindly work makes it glad.

Journal Reflections:

1. *How can you help someone else today? Reach out and offer a kind word to someone who may also be struggling.*

2. *Take a walk outside and breathe deeply. Enjoy nature's perfection.*

CHAPTER 15

But I Still Have a Few Questions

The doctors have been great about explaining the cancer, the treatments options, surgery outcomes and expected recovery. However, there are three burning questions that are left unanswered:

1. What did I do wrong to get cancer?
2. Are you sure there isn't any more cancer in another part of my body somewhere?
3. How can I make sure it doesn't return?

My logical brain knows there are not any scientific answers for these questions, but my emotional brain just will not accept that. There must be answers.

The emotional impact of hearing the words "you have cancer" is far reaching. My cancer doctor told me that the emotional healing would need as much, or more, attention that the physical healing, but I sure had no idea of what that really meant. Until now.

Now I understand.

People often experience a wide range of emotions with breast cancer and it was helpful to understand that my tidal waves of emotion were normal. That did not mean it would be easy, but it did mean that at least I was in good company.

I was experiencing the various stages of grief, and I was likely to bounce in and out of stages with varying levels of emotion.

These stages include:

1. Denial and Shock
2. Anger and Rage
3. Stress and Depression
4. Grief and Fear
5. Acceptance and Adjustment
6. Fight and Hope (this stage is specific to cancer patients)

Today, I was stuck in number two-Anger and Rage.

I am so angry and so scared. Cancer snuck up on me. I must be more vigilant. I can't let this happen again. I need help. I deserve answers.

I need someone to tell me how to get these thoughts out of my head before they drive me crazy with worry and anxiety. I know it's not logical, but cancer isn't logical either.

I still need the answers.

Healing Inspiration:

James 1: 56
But if any of you lacks wisdom, he should ask God
who gives to all generously and ungrudgingly, and
he will be given it. But he should ask in faith, not
doubting, for the one who doubts is like a wave of the
sea that is driven and tossed about by the wind.

Journal Reflections:

1. *Are you worried that you did something "wrong" to get*
   cancer? Speak to your doctor so he or she can help alleviate
   your worry.

2. *Reach out for help today. Ask for what you need to make*
   yourself feel strong and safe.

Part Three

Overwhelming Fear

CHAPTER 16

I Know You Think
God Isn't Listening

M y dad was sick for a long as I could remember. He struggled with heart issues, high blood pressure, and anxiety. He was a hardworking, hard-headed man who worked blue-collar jobs his entire life to provide for his large family. Every few years there was a traumatic event involving his health and we would be called to the hospital because of the grave nature of his health. Each time he pulled through. The doctors were always amazing at his ability to heal. We all knew it was his stubbornness that pulled him from the hands of death and that kept him fighting for another day.

But in August of 2010, he knew this time would be different. He had been in the hospital for several days and the medical staff was unsure of how to move forward. We had a Monday morning meeting with the hospital staff, and we talked about moving him to hospice because they felt there was nothing more they could do for him.

I went into the room to see my dad and I tried to comfort him as he thrashed in pain. He pulled me close to him and whispered, "it's time for me to go." I said "Dad, are you sure? Are you ready to go?" "Yes," he said, "I'm ready, I'm ready to go." "Ok, do you want us to help you?" I asked. "Yes, please help me. I'm done now. I'm ready to go" he said. "Ok, Dad, we will help. I will speak to the nurses and we will help you."

I left the room and met up with my sisters, my mom, and the head hospice nurse. I told them of the conversation I had just had with my dad and everything changed. Instead of the hospital and doctors fighting us to say there was "more to be done," they changed course and within hours we had a plan to admit my Dad into hospice. Once that happened, all medications would stop, and the natural course of death would take over.

My dad died within twenty-three hours of being admitted to hospice.

During his last hours, my sister and I had the privilege of being with him for hospice happy hour, which is a very beautiful thing for hospice patients. Each day the staff comes around and takes alcohol orders for patients and their visitors. We ordered a beer and although my dad was unconscious, we continued to talk to him as if he were awake and coherent. I told him we ordered a beer and we were going to enjoy happy- hour. We took a sponge and soaked it with the beer, and then held it to his lips and told him to take his drink. His lips grabbed the sponge and he sucked the beer from it and suddenly a smirky little smile came across his face. We laughed and enjoyed several more sips.

Less than two hours later, he died.

Fast forward several months and my life had entered a very dark and stormy phase. I was really struggling with life's challenges and I felt like I could barely make it through the day. I had to drag myself out of bed, try to look and behave in a positive manner, and work my way through this very dark phase. Every night I prayed to my Dad," *Please talk to God and send me some help. I need someone to take care of me. I'm not strong enough for this.*"

And then it happened.

I had the same dream over the course of several weeks. I was out to dinner with friends and there was laughter and fun. There, in the background, was my Dad. He was always just in the background. He never spoke or made himself known, he just lingered in the background giving me the "thumbs-up" with a big happy smile on his face. Each time this dream occurred, I would wake up and think, *Wow, I saw my Dad. That was cool.*

Time passed and then he came again. This time, I knew it was much more serious.

Growing up as young adults, whenever we were in trouble (well past the "spanking years"), my Dad would sit us down and try to reason with us with a stern speech about whatever topic we had just screwed up and he would redirect our thinking and straighten the path.

In this dream, it was just my Dad and me. No one else was around. I knew it was going to be one of those serious talks just by the tone of his voice. He sat me down and said, "I've heard your prayers. I know that you think God isn't listening, but that's not the case. It hurts me to see you struggle so much when you already have everything you need to get yourself through this dark part of your life. You are strong. You don't need someone to come and take care of you. You just need to take care of yourself. It's time to "get on with it." You deserve to be happy and you must do this for yourself. You have got to let go of the past and build a new future. No one can do this for you. You have got to do it for yourself."

I did not even get a chance to speak. The dream was over.

I woke up feeling very emotional. I was happy to have just seen my Dad again. I felt his presence so strong and I knew that he meant business. I felt scared to move forward but I also felt a strange surge of strength that I am sure came directly from heaven.

I knew what I had to do. No one could do this for me. I had to find the courage to do it for myself.

Cancer is the same lesson.

No one can do this for me. I must do it for myself. I must find the courage to pull myself through this storm.

Healing Inspiration:

Psalm 142: 7-8
Listen to my cry for help,
for I am brought very low.
Rescue me from my pursuers,
for they are too strong for me.
Lead me out of my prison,
that I may give thanks to your name.
Then the just shall gather around me
because you have been good to me.

Journal Reflections:

1. *When have you felt that God wasn't listening to your prayers?*

2. *How have you strengthened your trust in God?*

CHAPTER 17

Face the Storm Head On

My sister is a sailor and it is her sailing experience that helped pull me through my cancer storm.

For me, the mental toll of having breast cancer was stronger and deeper than my fear of its physical impacts. I was scared of the surgery, scars and recovery, but I was even more terrified of the mental impacts, because it seemed I didn't have control over when the waves of emotion came or for how long they stayed. It was all-consuming. All sorts of non-rational thoughts ran through my head. *How could I get them to go away?*

My sister told me that as part of becoming a certified sailor, you are taught to safely maneuver through unexpected storms while out at sea. That seemed like something I needed to learn.

She explained that when a storm approaches, you have two options to weather the storm; you can reef the main sail and jib to allow your boat to handle easier and safer, or if you determine you are going to sail through the storm, you should ensure all crew members are latched to the boat for maximum safety.

If the storm becomes too powerful, and your boat and crew are unsafe, you can "heave to" which means you turn the boat away from the wind, and then you turn your rudder and main sail toward the wind. These offsetting forces balance the boat and hold her steady in one position so you can "Ride out the Storm." The boat will remain safe while you wait for the storm to pass.

That was it. I needed to "heave to" and turn my boat away from the wind so I could safely ride out the storm. Now I knew what had to be done.

Once I learned how to be a sailor, I would mentally visualize the process each time my mind became entangled in an overwhelming storm. I would meditate and focus on what a sailor would do, heave to, lock your wheel or lash your rudder and ride out the storm.

Today I am a sailor. Today I feel safe.

Healing Inspiration:

Psalm 107: 28-31
In their distress they cried to the Lord,
who brought them out of their peril,
hushed the storm to a murmur;
the waves of the sea were stilled.
They rejoiced that the sea grew calm,
that God brought them to the harbor
they longed for.
Let them thank the Lord for such kindness,
such wondrous deeds for mere mortals.

Journal Reflections:

1. *Have you ever experienced a catastrophic storm like a hurricane or tornado? How did it make you feel?*

2. *What scares you most today? Write down your feelings and honor them.*

CHAPTER 18

In This (Dreadful) Moment

I am learning so much about the absolute strength of fear and how it can crush the joy from your life. I am learning to honor fear and learn from its power.

Fear happens every day to everybody and it is often the result of our mind fixating on images of an undesirable situation that "might" happen to us in the future.

But this fear feels different. This fear is not so much about what might happen in the future, it is more about what is happening now. Each day of my cancer journey has been different with some good days and some bad days. It seems though, that when the bad days come, they are darker and more intense than any fear I have experienced so far.

When you read about how to conquer fear, experts say we should develop a positive attitude and create visualizations and affirmations to help eliminate the specific fear. All that is easier said than done, but I am going to keep trying.

Today, I am fighting to stay positive. I am turning my boat toward the storm and will ride out these brutal waves. Instead of fighting so strongly to beat my fear, I have decided to honor it as a valid feeling and the refocus my emotions toward hope, joy, and happiness.

Today, I am not as terrified as I was yesterday. Today, I am staying positive.

For the first time since my diagnosis, I feel a hint of excitement. I feel strong enough to look beyond the pain of surgery and recovery and focus on the joy and happiness that is part of my life.

Healing Inspiration:

Isaiah 41: 10
Fear not, I am with you;
be not dismayed; I am your God.
I will strengthen you, and help you,
and uphold you with my right hand of justice.

Journal Reflections:

1. *Clear your mind and meditate with the clear intention that God has you in his hands. You are safe and you are loved.*

2. *Think about your life "after cancer". What makes you most excited? Look forward to those days; they will be here soon.*

CHAPTER 19

Today is a Cancer-Free Day

After my diagnosis, it seemed that the only thing anyone wanted to talk about was cancer. My cancer, their friend's, mom's, dad's, brother's, sister's cancer, a breakthrough they just read about, what I should eat, what I should not eat, and on and on. Everybody had a story or a solution or both.

After a few weeks of this pattern, I began to declare certain days "Cancer-Free". On these days, there was no talk of cancer. I tried not to think about cancer. I tried to pretend that I was living my "pre-cancer" life. I told my friends and family of my new Cancer-Free Days and if someone called to talk about it, I would politely let them know that they had picked a Cancer-Free Day and that I was not going to talk about it today.

These Cancer-Free Days became very comforting. These days gave me strength to get through all the other days. I knew that I would need an extra boost of strength for what was ahead of me. On my Cancer-Free Days, I could go back to being normal. I could be ME and just do whatever I wanted. I did not have to be a breast cancer patient.

I was gaining strength. I was determined to not let cancer define me. I found an awesome saying online that I would repeat to myself often, "My illness does not define me. My strength and courage do."

I took back my control and decided when I would and would not talk about cancer. It did not take away the problem, but it felt awful good to have a little bit of control.

Go ahead, make today a Cancer-Free Day. You deserve it.

Healing Inspiration:

Matthew 7: 7-8
"Ask and it will be given to you; seek and you will find;
knock and the door will be opened to you. For everyone
who asks receives; and the one who seeks, finds; and
to the one who knocks, the door will be opened."

Journal Reflections:

1. *Celebrate today. It is a Cancer-Free Day! How are you*
    managing to keep today Caner-Free?

2. *Have some fun; go shopping, call a friend, do whatever will*
    help you forget about cancer.

It Won't Always Be This Hard

Thirty days ago, I was diagnosed with cancer. Hearing those words instantly sent me to a new place. *I am now one of them. I am now a cancer patient.*

Yesterday I had to go for a CT scan and my emotions came spilling out as I sat in the reception area waiting my turn. I thought was getting stronger, but the ever-present what-if game began running through my head again, and this time with a real vengeance.

What if they found more cancer somewhere else in my body? What if there was more bad news?

Breast cancer snuck up on me, and I was now scared to death that it would be in another part of my body. From research, I understood the high correlation between breast, lung, and ovarian cancer, and I was terrified that today they would find the cancer again.

As they turned on the machine and asked me if I was ready to go, I started to cry. *Yes, I'm ready, but can you please hurry?* I closed my eyes and repeated the Hail Mary as many times as it took to get me through the test. That was so scary.

What if they give me more bad news? I didn't know cancer was in my body in the first place, so how could I be sure it wasn't going to attack somewhere else? The fear overwhelmed me again, suddenly and with great power.

It is always about the fear. How does one get through their cancer journey without being completely terrified?

Fear seems to be like a spoiled child. If you don't give it attention when it demands it, things spiral out of control and the fear gets louder and louder until you finally have to stand face-to-face and address the issue.

Please stop it. Fear, you will not win. I will win.

I will honor your presence and give you a few moments to throw your little tantrum, but then we are done.

As the CT machine's motor shut off, I remembered my meditation and affirmations and quickly begin to calm my fear. It takes every ounce of my energy to wrestle with this monster, but I did it! I am done with the test.

A friend reminded me yesterday of this saying - "you never know how strong you are until being strong is the only choice you have".

Yes, that is true, it is the only choice I have. I will be strong.

Healing Inspiration:

Psalm 56: 4-5
When I am afraid, in you I place my trust.
God, I praise your promise; in you I trust,
I do not fear.
What can mere flesh do to me?

Journal Reflections:

1. *Can you feel that your cancer journey is making you a stronger person? How has it changed who you are?*

2. *Thank God for giving you strength and courage as you fight through this storm.*

CHAPTER 21

How Bad is This Going to Hurt?

Today I met with my "plastic guy", my awesome doctor who is going to rebuild my chest and give me new boobs. It was a long appointment because we had a lot to talk about.

The surgery would take between twelve-fourteen hours and he would make an incision just below my belly button from hip to hip. He would transfer the tissue (aka fat) from my stomach to my chest.

I heard the words and I understood the surgical procedure, but I did not have a grasp of how much it would hurt. Cutting me from hip to hip sounded awful. Cutting my boobs off sounded awful. I had never experienced a chronic condition or had a major surgery, so I had no compass for which to gauge this upcoming pain.

I went to my ladies. My Pink Sisters would know the answers. They were there to help me understand.

I went to the discussion board on breastcancer.org and searched for the DIEP surgery. I read every single post – the good, the bad and the ugly. There was so much information and I could not take it in fast enough. This was great. It was like one big library of cancer stuff. I posted my questions and excitedly looked for responses from my fellow warriors. They would tell me. They knew what to expect.

Within minutes I started to receive responses from ladies who had done similar surgeries. It was so helpful to hear the real story, and to be able to prepare in this way. Obviously, each person handles pain differently and everyone heals on their own timeline, but it was so helpful to read everything that was posted by those who had gone before me. *Thank you, my Pink Sisters.*

It felt so comforting. My ladies were there for me. This was something I could trust. They sent words of encouragement and love. I didn't personally know these ladies, but there is such a strong level of support and comradery in the cancer community, that I felt like I had known my new friends for years. It was so comforting.

Healing Inspiration:

Isaiah 66: 13
As a mother comforts her son,
so will I comfort you;
in Jerusalem you shall find your comfort.

Journal Reflections:

1. *How are you feeling today? Are the feelings of anger and sadness beginning to subside?*

2. *Find a quiet place and meditate on the belief that the universe is sending you positive energy and a great big hug. Everything is going to be OK.*

Part Four

Surgery Day

CHAPTER 22

Tokens of Closeness

A s I prepared for surgery, I wanted to feel close to my family. I needed to feel safe and protected. I was so afraid of leaving them and never coming back, and I could not shake this ever-present wave of terror.

I wore a necklace that was very meaningful to me with important mementoes that carried special meaning. On my necklace, I wore a cross that was blessed by Pope John Paul II, a Blessed Mary Medal (known as the Miraculous Medal) and two baby rings to represent my beautiful children. These small, but very special tokens, made me feel safe and strong.

This was my magic necklace, a bit like Harry Potter's invisibility cloak or Frodo's magic ring. When I wore my necklace, nothing bad could hurt me. With it, I would be safe and protected. During my tests and at every step along the way when I felt sad or scared, I would reach for those special tokens and say a prayer to God to bring to strength.

I wore the necklace from the day I was diagnosed, and I still wear it today. It reminds me that I am stronger than I realize and that I can accomplish anything.

Make yourself a necklace of closeness. What you put on the necklace is up to you. They are personal tokens that mean the most to you. What makes you feel strong? What gives you strength?

Of course, I could not wear the necklace during surgery, but I wore it until they made me take it off and then I carefully placed it in my purse, so I knew where it was and so I could put it on again as soon as I woke up from surgery.

I knew it would make me strong. I felt safe.

Healing Inspiration:

Luke 12: 34
For where your treasure is,
there also will your heart be.

Journal Reflections:

1. *What tokens have you chosen to take with you to the hospital?*

2. *Know that your family and friends love you and that you are not alone. Be strong and be brave.*

CHAPTER 23

Anti-Bacterial Soap

T oday the hospital called, and the nurse carefully walked me through the pre-surgery checklist and made sure I was writing everything down. She kept asking me, "Are you writing this down?" "Can you repeat back to me what I just told you?" *Yes, I'm writing it down. I hate every word you are telling me, but yes, I am writing it down.* Then she followed up with an email of the detailed list of what I could and could not do prior to surgery.

Wow, it was quite a list.

It started with instructions to stop taking over-the-counter medications, vitamins, and Ibuprofen immediately. I was to stop eating certain foods and not eat after a certain time the evening before surgery.

On the morning of the surgery, there would be no water, no food, and no breath mints. Oh my gosh, it made me laugh when they said no breath mints. *How could that be important enough to make the pre-surgery list? How could that matter in the least?* I had no idea breath mints could be so impactful and that they were banned as part of the pre-surgery checklist. I could not stop laughing every time I read that part of the instructions.

Then there was the anti-bacterial soap. The nurse must have said this part ten times. She made such a big deal about making sure I had purchased anti-bacterial soap. Regular soap would not do – it had to be antibacterial soap.

She explained the showering process to me in what felt like excruciating detail. *Come on lady, I know how to take a shower. And yes, I was still writing all of this down.* I was to take at least a twenty-minute shower, soap, rinse, soap rinse again. It was very important; nothing shorter than twenty minutes. There was to be no skimping. She reiterated these instructions in her very serious, stern, "I am not joking" nurse voice. She was scaring me.

OK. I was ready to go. I knew what had to be done.

Isn't it funny that whenever someone tells you that you can't have something, even if you haven't had it for months, you suddenly develop an urge for it?! For me, it was that darn breath mint.

I followed the nurse's directions to a T, but honestly, all I could think of in the morning before I headed off to the hospital was that darn breath mint. A breath mint sounded perfect right now.

I really wanted a breath mint!

Healing Inspiration:

Romans 16: 13
May the God of hope fill you with all joy and peace
in believing, so that you may abound in hope by the
power of the Holy Spirit.

Journal Reflections:

1. *By now, everything is nearly complete. There are a few final steps of preparation. How does this make you feel?*

2. *Breathe deeply. Close your eyes and breathe. You are strong and you are a warrior.*

CHAPTER 24

Happy Cancer-Eve

E verything is done. The rest is up to God.

It has been a busy time making sure all my tasks are complete ahead of my upcoming surgery. Remember, I am a strong Type A with control issues, so I have handled my surgery preparations as I would for any other important work project. Organize and plan. Plan and organize.

But now there was nothing left to do but hand it over to God. I was scared. Really scared. I prayed:

> *Dear God, please hold my hand and see me through a successful surgery. Guide my doctors with a steady hand, a clear mind and an open heart. Give courage to those tasked with waiting and peace to those feeling extra worried. Thank you for helping me to find this cancer in its early stage and for all the love and support from friends and family around the globe.*
>
> *In Jesus' name, Amen.*

The day was done and now I needed to sleep. It was my last night before losing my boobs, but I did not look at it that way. For me at that moment, it was my last night with cancer in my body. *Tomorrow, this monster will be gone. Tomorrow my life will be forever changed.*

I knew that it was so important for me to go into surgery with as positive of an attitude as I could manage. I practiced my meditation and prayed until the sun came up. There was no sleep. I could do that for the fourteen hours in surgery.

Please keep me safe. Please bring me back home to my family.

Healing Inspiration:

John 6: 37
Everything that the Father gives me will come to me,
and I will not reject anyone who comes to me, because
I came down from heaven not to do my own will but
the will of the one who sent me.

Journal Reflections:

1. *Close your eyes and thank God for making you a strong warrior. Write down your feelings and ask him to take them from you today so that you can focus on healing.*

2. *You are almost there! You can do it. Stay strong.*

Leaving Home at 4 a.m.

The anticipation was almost over.

The alarm went off at 3:00 am. I am not sure why I thought I needed an hour to get ready since I was dressed and ready to go in 15 minutes. Now, I had forty-five minutes left to ponder. That was not a good plan; there was way too much time to ponder.

All I could think about was what I could not have. *I am thirsty and I am hungry. I should have eaten more for dinner last night. I cannot survive without a glass of water, right now.*

My mind was racing, and I could not calm myself done. I have never been so anxious in my life.

I prayed to God. I prayed that he would hold my hand through the long fourteen-hour surgery and bring me back to my girls. I prayed that he would give me courage to fight hard while the doctors were busy removing the cancer.

I was scared.

During this time, I knew it was important for me to get a grip. I had to summons all my inner strength to force myself to calm down and to clear my mind of worry. I did not want to "go under" being scared. I wanted to think happy thoughts and relax.

Time to breathe. Long breath in…..long breath out. Keep going.

74 | GERI MARONEY

Healing Inspiration:

John 14: 1
Do not let your hearts be troubled. You have faith in God;
have faith also in me.

Journal Reflections:

1. *Be gentle and kind to yourself. If you feel afraid, it's OK.*

2. *Think of a time when you were happiest in your life. Hold those thoughts and bring them with you to surgery. It's a good day!*

CHAPTER 26

Big and Brave

I remember when my girls were little, I tried to teach them to be "big and brave." When they would come from school and be sad about something that had happened, I always tried to show them that they had more inner courage than they thought they did. When they we too afraid to try something new, I would tell them that they could conquer whatever challenge they faced. They just needed to be "big and brave." We always talked about being "big and brave."

Now it was my turn. Today it was my lesson to learn.

With nowhere else to turn, I had to face the fact that I was the only one who could muster the courage to pull myself through this. No one could do it for me. It was all me.

There was nothing left to do, but to be big and brave.

It was 5 a.m., and all the pre-surgery preparations were complete. I was wrapped in my lovely blue hospital gown with those cool yellow non-skid socks. The IV had been started and I just waiting for my name to be called to head into surgery.

Suddenly, the power went out. I kid you not. The surgery waiting area went dark. Because of the hospital generators, it came back on very quickly, but holy moly. That felt like a sign that I should not go forward with this fourteen-hour surgery.

It felt like God telling me to STOP.

Of course, we could not stop. The loss of electricity felt like a metaphor for the way my spirit felt at that moment. Depleted and dark.

Within a short period of time everything was back online my doctor stuck his head into my room and said, "Are you ready to go? We are fifteen minutes till game time." *OMG.... What? Fifteen minutes? No no no. I'm not big and brave yet.* I felt a new, very powerful surge of fear. Please give me a few more minutes.

It was then that I closed my eyes and blocked everything else out. I sat with my breath and just wiped everything else from my mind. I remembered my girls as little ones and remembered telling them, "It's ok. You just have to be big and brave. You can do it. I love you and I know you can do. Just be big and brave."

The medical team arrived, and everyone was ready to go. They wheeled me down the hall to surgery. My surgeon leaned his head very close to mine and said "Try to relax. I promise I will take good care of you."

Wish me luck.

Healing Inspiration:

Psalm 31: 25
Be strong and take heart, all you who hope in the Lord.

Journal Reflections:

1. *Close your eyes and breathe. Be proud of the courage you have displayed and know that God is watching over you today.*

2. *You are a strong warrior. Your family and friends love you and God loves you too. You've got this! You are beating cancer!*

Part Five

Physical Healing

CHAPTER 27

Waking Up

I remember waking up.

I remember thanking God for helping me through this terrible ordeal. It had been, as they said it would be, a fourteen-hour surgery. My doctor was there with me as they wheeled me into my recovery room. She said everything went well and that I did a great job. *I am so thirsty; can someone please give me some ice chips?*

My next stop was ICU. I would spend three or four days in ICU and then another one or two days in a regular room before I could be released to go home.

Being in ICU sounded so scary. When someone is in the Intensive Care Unit it is always serious. This was serious. There were so many tubes come from my body and the machines were beeping like crazy. But I wasn't scared anymore. I was relieved to have this part of my journey over with, and I knew my team of doctors and nurses would watch me closely and keep me safe.

I was bandaged very tight across both my chest and my abdomen. But the chest pain was excruciating and scary. *Ok doc, I know you said I would experience pain, but wow, this is some heavy-duty pain.* The nerve damage from my double mastectomy was excruciating. I felt like I was having a heart attack. It came on fast and strong and it scared me. *How could I die of a heart attack after surviving a fourteen-hour cancer surgery?*

My doctor sat with me and explained that the nerves would do this from time to time over the course of the next many months. In some cases, it could take up to a year to heal. But that is why I was in ICU, so that they could watch things closely and make sure I was healing properly. *Ok, that helped a lot. Thank you for explaining those details.*

I had been out of surgery for a very short time and I had learned my first post-cancer lesson. When the pain comes, I have the power to contain it and soften my panic. I will continue to quickly remind myself that I am fine and that I am not having a heart attack. It is just nerve pain.

There is no need to panic.

The mind is the strongest muscle in the body, and according to statistics, produces over 60,000 thoughts every day. The mind is constantly sensing, perceiving, retrieving, and storing data to keep you at the top of your game.

However, in the case of cancer, the mind senses, perceives, retrieves, and stores data that is not valuable to your healing.

I need to find a way to distract my mind. Everything is going to be ok.

Healing Inspiration:

Psalm 27: 1
The Lord is my light and my salvation;
whom do I fear?
The Lord is my life's refuge;
of whom am I afraid.

Journal Reflections:

1. *How is your pain level today? What techniques can you follow to help you breathe through the pain?*

2. *Stay strong, my fellow warrior. Each day will get better. May God give you strength today.*

CHAPTER 28

The 2:37a.m. Storm

I t is 2:37 a.m. on the morning of Day Four post-surgery, and I am having an absolute meltdown. I am still in ICU and the medications have worn off. I must wait a little longer before my next dose and I am trying hard to meditate to keep from going insane.

Every night since surgery, I wake up around 2:30 a.m. with a very strong wave of emotions. I have come to affectionately call this time "The Storm."

The Storm is powerful and demanding. It crashes with waves of fear and doubt, until finally my heart feels completely overwhelmed. My sense of safety is shattered (again), and I wonder if I will ever be strong again.

Since this has happened multiple times, I have learned a few tips of how best to get through "The Storm." I reach for my headphones and turn on my meditation music that includes sounds from my favorite place – the beach. I listen to the waves and the birds and pretend that I am far away from this hospital bed.

After a few nights of this ritual, I see the night nurse peeking into my room to check on me. I see her standing there watching me with my headphones on at 2:30 in the morning. She smiles at me and I wave back.

I remember what my sister taught me. I remember about being a sailor. It is time to put on my captain's hat and hold on tight. It is time to be a sailor and turn my ship's hull toward the storm. It is time to batten down the hatches. I must ride-it-out and I am determined to focus on the positive. But I need your help.

I need you to shine your flashlight of love and encouragement my way so that I can steer my ship through the storm to safety. Please shine your flashlight and show me the way.

In the morning, before my nurse left her shift, she came to my room and sat down next to me on my bed. She took my hand and said, "I know that you have been waking up in the middle of the night, and I know that you are scared, but there are many people in your life who love you and who will help you though this." She continued, "You remind me so much of my own mother and my heart hurts for what you have had to endure. Your strength is obvious to me and I know that you will conquer this."

Tears were streaming down both of our faces. I did not know this woman, except as my "night nurse". Her name was Shannon, and she was so much more than my night nurse. On that day, she was my angel.

Healing Inspiration:

Psalm 46: 2-4
God is our refuge and our strength,
an ever-present help in distress.
Thus we do not fear, though earth be shaken
and mountains quake to the depths of the sea,
though its waters rage and foam
and mountains tetter at its surging,
The Lord of hosts is with us;
our stronghold is the God of Jacob.

Journal Reflections:

1. *What are your strongest thoughts today? Write them down and release the emotions around them. Clear your mind.*

2. *What can others do for you to help alleviate your pain and worry?*

CHAPTER 29

Homecoming

I made it. Five days in intensive care and one day on the regular floor and I am finally being released from the hospital. I am so happy to be leaving this place.

The patient release process took more than an hour with most of that time spent at the pharmacy with the six medication prescriptions that would now be very important to my pain management plan.

I have tubes coming out of my body, two across my chest and two across my abdomen. *Ugh. I already hate these tubes, they hurt, and they are gross.*

But I am home, and it feels like such a relief.

The next stage of my cancer journey has just begun. Now, my primary job was to nurture myself and heal.

When I got home, I went straight to bed. I love my bed. I feel safe, warm, and protected in my own bed. Don't we all? When things are toughest, isn't it comforting to just crawl into bed and pull the covers up? Metaphorically, it shuts the world out, even if it is just for a little while.

I am ready to shut the world out for a little while. I am happy to be home. *Thank you, God, for watching over me throughout this very difficult journey. Please continue to place your guiding hands over me and help me heal. In Jesus' name, Amen.*

Healing Inspiration:

Jeremiah 17: 14
Heal me, Lord, that I may be healed;
save me, that I may be saved,
for it is you whom I praise.

Journal Reflections:

1. *Congratulations, beautiful warrior, the worst part is over and now it is time to heal. Rest easy and be gentle to yourself.*

2. *What would make you smile today? Tell someone what you need and ask them to help you smile!*

CHAPTER 30

Are You Kidding Me?

There is much to be said for pain medication. They keep you numb from the pain and from reality. *The reality is that I have four drains coming from my body, one scar from hip-to-hip and another across each boob. It looks like I have been sliced in half.*

But, when I look at the progress I have made, I know that I should be thankful. I am thankful - very thankful.

But, today is not a good day. I am mad and disgusted. *This sucks. These drains are disgusting and annoying.* I can't shower because I am too weak to stand up for that long. Even if I could, I can't shower because these body drains are so cumbersome. And draining the drains? No way. That is the grossest thing ever. It is necessary and nonnegotiable, but it is gross.

I am not sleeping well because I must lay on my back propped by pillows or risk a blood clot from the drain areas.

Oh, and I can't eat because I can't properly digest food because of the high level of pain medications. Everything is out of whack. *My body is struggling to function as usual; my mind is mush and these drains are really pissing me off.*

Maybe tomorrow will be a better day.

Healing Inspiration:

Isaiah 43:2-3
Fear not, for I have redeemed you;
I have called you by name: you are mine.
When you pass through the water, I will be with you;
Ii the rivers you shall not drown.
When you walk through fire, you shall not be burned;
the flames shall not consume you.

Journal Reflections:

1. *Are you noticing a difference in your pain level? What is your biggest struggle with your recovery?*

2. *What are you most thankful for today? Thank God for all that you have.*

CHAPTER 31

Prune Juice and The Price is Right

My recovery continues. Some days are great. Some days are not. It feels like one step forward and two steps back, but I keep telling myself that at least I am stepping forward.

My emotions are calming down a bit and there are not quite as many unexplained meltdowns. It is so weird. I am fine one minute and a complete ball of mush the next. There is no real reason, it just happens.

Week two of recovery has developed its own routine. After a night of restless sleep, it's time for breakfast and pain medication, physical therapy with breathing exercises and then a morning stroll, which consists of fifteen-twenty minutes of walking around the house or out onto the patio and down the steps to the backyard.

I just need to keep moving and I need to push myself further a little every day. I am proud of my progress, and I am determined to stay positive along this journey.

After breakfast, breathing exercises and walking, it is time for the best part of my morning - an ice-cold glass of prune juice and the latest episode of The Price is Right!! Haha.

Never in a million years would I have imagined that I would celebrate such a simple task list. Sometimes I laugh at myself. The Strong Type A in me thinks I have lost my mind, and that I should be doing more to push myself harder.

But no, not this time around. Cancer demands change. For me, this is one of the lessons I was meant to learn. The lesson of "doing nothing." Learning to do nothing is a big accomplishment for me.

Nothing is good. Nothing is perfect.

Here's to prune juice and The Price is Right!

Healing Inspiration:

Psalm 116: 6
The Lord protects the simple;
I was helpless, but God saved me.

Journal Reflections:

1. *Do you have trouble "doing nothing"? What steps can you take to practice this important skill?*

2. *Find time to meditate today. Clear your mind and feel the comfort of being "still". Give yourself this gift and practice it often.*

CHAPTER 32

1008 Hours of Pain

I magine this, you wake up to the pain, you go to sleep with the pain. It is with you every hour of every day.

For 1008 hours (forty-two days), that has been my life. Maybe I am a baby, but to me the pain has been excruciating. It is the price I am paying to be cancer free, and I will definitely take the trade, but it does not make it easy.

The pain has been exhausting and it often leaves me feeling completely fatigued. Even if we ignore the pain mentally, our bodies have to cope with the stimulation of pain signals. I have learned a very tough lesson in the power of pain.

But, today is the first day that I can feel a difference. Today, I feel like the pain is subsiding. It is no longer unbearable all of the time, it is only unbearable some of the time. I can see the light at the end of the tunnel.

Today, for the first time since my surgery, I am looking forward to getting back to life. I am looking forward to my new life from the lens of a cancer survivor. I have promised myself this change. I have earned this change.

This is another lesson I have learned. I have learned that I can start each day thinking of what I "want" to do, instead of what I "have" to do. You should try it. You don't need to be a cancer survivor to exercise this right, you can start your day with the freedom of choice.

Choose more of what you want to do and less of what others dictate to you. Do not wait until you have to endure 1008 hours of excruciating pain to be reminded of this life lesson.

Start today.

Healing Inspiration:

Ephesians: 1: 17-18
That the God of our Lord Jesus Christ, the Father of glory, may give you a spirit of wisdom and revelation resulting in knowledge of him. May the else of your hearts be enlightened, that you may know what is the hope that belongs to his call, what are the riches of glory in his inheritance among the holy ones.

Journal Reflections:

1. *If you had to wipe the slate clean and define your "new life", what would it look like?*

2. *What changes can you make to draw yourself closer to this "new life"?*

CHAPTER 33

Lean on Me

I have always been the strong one. I have been the one that other people come to for help and support. I have rarely needed support from others. Actually, I have learned throughout my cancer journey that I have probably needed support many times in my past, but I was too proud, too stubborn or too busy to ask for support. For some reason, I had always felt that asking for support made me look weak.

However, there is a difference between being independent and knowing when you need help from others. It is not an all-or-nothing option. Just because I am independent, does not mean that I should not give myself a break and take help from others.

I don't have to be everything to everybody every minute of every day. That is too much pressure for anyone.

But that has been my modus operandi. I misinterpreted the goal. I thought that it was a "more is better" strategy. If I was independent to begin with, then the more independent I became the better I would be. I was wrong.

This is another lesson I have learned because of my cancer journey. I can lean on others. I must learn to lean on others. In time of crisis, we can learn to lean on one another and stand tall. Together we are stronger and together we can help each other through any storm. Our family and friends can make us stronger.

I must loosen my gripe and let other people help me. I must learn to lean on others.

I will lean on you and you can lean on me.

Healing Inspiration:

Proverbs 6: 27
Can a man take fire to his bosom,
and his garments not be burned?

Journal Reflections:

1. *When have you tried to be "all things to all people?*

2. *What are YOUR wants and needs? Are you fulfilling them first?*

CHAPTER 34

Scars

I have never had a scar. No broken bones and no significant wound. Now, it is different. Now I have major scars from hip to hip and across my chest. I have a significant wound and it is not just physical, it is also psychological.

I continue to feel very sad. and I mourn the loss of my pre-cancer life. But I am also focused on the future. I know that I will get stronger. My body has been rebuilt and my scars are healing.

It has taken me a little time, but I am beginning to view my physical scars as a success, as my personal badge of courage. *My battle wounds prove that I was stronger than cancer. I won. The cancer is gone.*

But the fight was not without casualty. My body is forever scarred, and my confidence and emotional strength continues to elude me. I am still struggling with fear that comes at unexpected times. *What is wrong with me? Why can't I finally get over this?*

I feel strong for a period of days and then wham, it comes back. The fear is back, and I can't hold things together. I don't feel like I can hold my progress. I feel like instead of one step forward and two steps back, it is a half-step forward and three steps back.

But today I am setting aside my fight with fear to celebrate my scars. My scars represent my own imperfections. They remind me of the pain, lose and transformation that cancer has brought to my life. They remind me that there is so much more to my life on the other side of the fear that scares me today. They remind me to be "big and brave".

To every cancer warrior reading this book, congratulations, you did it! You are stronger today than when you began your journey and you will continue to build your strength each day going forward. Your scars are your trophy. You are a beautiful warrior.

Congratulations!

Healing Inspiration:

Exodus 14: 2
My strength and my courage is the Lord,
and he had been my savior.
He is my God, I praise him;
The God of my father, I extol him.

Journal Reflections:

1. *You did it; you are a beautiful warrior! Celebrate your success. Celebrate your scars and your journey.*

2. *Take care of your new body and honor your scars. They mark a very important journey, my dear warrior.*

CHAPTER 35

Nipple Tattoos

Today I got nipple tattoos. It makes me laugh every time I say those words. Never in my life would I have imagined that statement coming from my mouth. Nipple tattoos? Really?

Yes. Nipple tattoos. Beautiful nipple tattoos.

Nipple tattoos gave me back some of what cancer took away. Cancer mutilated my body and the simple process of nipple tattoos helped me heal a sadness that I have felt since the day after my surgery.

Getting tattoos helped me to be able to look into the mirror and see a whole person again. When I started my cancer journey, I underestimated the emotional impact it would have. I did not think that losing my boobs would make me feel so sad.

So, here it was, the day I would get to complete you new look. I was excited and nervous. But here we go.

It was a funny day. It was hilarious. My sister came with me to be my Nipple Consultant. We laughed before even getting to the doctor's office about the idea of actually getting nipple tattoos. It seemed surreal.

It was a two-hour appointment with the first hour filled with decisions that included nipple placement, size, color, contouring and shading. *Oh my gosh. I had no idea there were so many details.* We laughed but this was serious business! As my doctor kept telling us, "nobody wants pepperonis" for nipples." *Yes, that would be true, for sure. No pepperonis for me, please!*

Ok, all the decisions had been made, let the tattooing commence.

It was an emotional day. Another step toward healing.

My beautiful nipple tattoos.

Healing Inspiration:

Journal Reflections:

1. *God sees your beauty. You are perfect in every way. Can you see it? How are you feeling about yourself today?*

2. *Reach out to someone who may need your help today. Help spread your strength.*

Part Six

The Mental Aftermath

CHAPTER 36

PTSD – The New Enemy

After my first post-op follow up appointment, the doctor asked me a new set of questions, including things like: 1) are you feeling sad or full of dread?, 2) do you think about hurting yourself or others?, 3) are you feeling overwhelmed?

At first, I thought it was weird that he would ask me these kinds of questions. I did not think much about it and said everything was fine and that I was not feeling that way.

But, with the next appointment it was completely different. I had to admit that I was feeling many of those emotions. I was overwhelmed, and I had unbearable feelings of sadness and dread. I would wake up in the morning and count the hours until I could go back to bed at night. I was very depressed.

Everything felt over-exaggerated. I felt emotionally weak and I was scared that I might not recover. The physical healing was well underway, so why was I now taking such a nose-dive in the area of mental health? It didn't seem fair.

According to research done by the Columbia University's College of Physicians & Surgeons, nearly one in four cancer survivors met the criteria for PTSD, which includes symptoms such as:

- Panic attacks (both isolated and chronic), which include a racing heartbeat, trembling or shortness of breath
- Avoidance of follow-up checkups and other appointments, or anything you associate with your cancer or treatment
- Feeling hyper-alert, almost like you are on watch for something

- Worry that any change in your body means your cancer has returned
- Feeling jumpy or easily startled
- Unexplainable irritability
- Difficulty concentrating
- Trouble falling or staying asleep
- Frequent nightmares or flashbacks

Great, now I had to worry about surviving PTSD? How long was I going to be this way? How long would I have to struggle to conquer these hypersensitive emotions? Could I trust myself? I was terrified all over again.

My dear cancer warrior, if you are feeling these symptoms, talk to your doctor. Don't wait until the feelings escalate and become unmanageable. This is just another step in our healing process, and it is important to recognize and address these symptoms.

Give yourself credit; you beat the biggest monster of all - you beat CANCER, and now, you need to be gentle with yourself as you work through the after-affects.

My doctor confirmed that I was suffering from PTSD from cancer and suggested that I start journaling to help get my feeling outs. Together, we created a plan to help me find healthy ways to work through the triggers.

It is not really a monster; it is just a shadow.

Remember to be "big and brave." You are going to be OK.

Healing Inspiration:

Matthew 19: 26
Jesus looked at them and said, "For human beings this is impossible, but for God all things are possible."

Journal Reflections:

1. *Hold on, my sweet warrior; I know these feelings of fear, anxiety and anger are difficult to handle, but they won't last forever. Write down how you are feeling and think of ways you can help yourself feel safe. It is going to be OK.*

2. *Reach out to others day. Ask for what you need and be gentle with yourself. This is another important step in your healing process.*

CHAPTER 37

The Power of Anger

Today I woke up knowing that I had to travel for business. I am feeling particularly angry, but I cannot identify any one reason for the anger. *Ok, try to relax and keep your heart open today and see what the world brings.* Then, I got out of bed and began my journey.

I left for the airport as usual and made my way through security on to the train to the terminal. When I travel, I don't usually pay much attention to the people around me. I just keep my eyes focused forward and get to where I need to be.

But today it felt different. Today I noticed an older woman making her way toward me as the train approached the platform. We both boarded at the same time and I went to the back of the train as I always did. She followed and stood next to me. I could see her out of the corner of my eye but did not take time to make eye contact.

She turned to me asked how my day was going. I said, "Good, how are you today?" She said she was having a great day and that she was so excited to be traveling to see her daughter. "We haven't spoken in many years", she said. "We let anger build up and it destroyed our relationship."

"I'm sorry," I said, but I didn't engage much further in the conversation. She moved closer toward me and went on to explain that her daughter called her out-of-the-blue and apologized for the past hurts they had endured and she invited her to come and join them at a family event that weekend.

Her words touched a nerve. I thought about the anger I had felt when I woke up that morning and tears began to well up in my eyes. I looked at this stranger, and she had tears in her eyes too.

She touched my arm and said "Don't let anger build up, don't let it take the joy from your life. Forgive others and forgive yourself."

Fighting back more tears, I smiled at her and thanked her for being my angel. I told her that those were the exact words I needed to hear on that day. I thanked her for her kind words and wished her well on her journey. She was so happy.

The train arrived at my stop and I had to get off. I remember exiting the train and looking back at her as I headed toward the escalator. She was smiling and waving to me as the train pulled away. I waved back and wiped away my tears.

Wow. What a gift.

It was such an important lesson for me that day. I had gotten out of balance and with the help of a stranger, I was very quickly brought back to center!

It was such an important lesson. Don't let anger build up, and don't let it take joy from your life. Forgive others and forgive yourself.

Thank you, my dear angel.

Healing Inspiration:

Mark 11: 25
When you stand to pray, forgive anyone against whom you have a grievance, so that your heavenly Father may in turn forgive you your transgressions.

Journal Reflections:

1. *What chance-encounter have you had that brought you a special message from heaven? How did it make you feel?*

2. *Have you released your anger? If not, try it and write down how you feel after "the release".*

CHAPTER 38

The Power of Fear

I have worked as a business executive for more a very long time and I have traveled the world. During one trip, I literally went around the world in eight days. It was a dreadfully tiring trip, but I did not want to be away from my family any longer than necessary, so I endured the inconvenience to get home as soon as possible.

Back then my motto was "work hard, play hard", and I always made sure to enjoy as much adventure as the schedule would allow. Work first and then play, but I always made sure to have time for fun. I remember golfing in Sydney, tango dancing in Buenos Aries and whiskey tasting in Dublin. I had staff in each location and over the years we had become more like family.

I have never had a phobia and have never shied away from a challenge. But after cancer, my business trips were different. I had suddenly developed a fear of flying. Prior to cancer, flying was like second nature, but now it was hard for me to get on the plane. It was bizarre and I wasn't sure where this new fear was coming from. *What if something bad happens? No one will be there to help me. No one will even know I am gone.*

My thoughts were not rational. Even though I was a single empty-nester, there were people in my life who knew where I was and who cared what happened to me. There really wasn't anything to be afraid of.

But as I struggled with the emotional aftereffects of cancer, I learned that an important step in conquering fear was to highlight the perceived concern and evaluate it logically. Here is what I was afraid of:

- What if I get sick?
- What if someone kidnaps me?
- What if I lose my passport or other identification?

Read my list. It's silly, right? Silly or not, this new fear was causing an intense surge of anxiety and I knew it must be addressed.

I am healthy and have no fact-based reason to worry about getting sick. The odds of being kidnapped are extremely remote. What if I lose my passport or ID? So, what, I wouldn't die. I can go to the appropriate agency for assistance and get a new one. It might cause delay and inconvenience, but I wouldn't die. It's not a big deal and it isn't something that should overshadow my travels.

This was another lesson. Fear can be a debilitating emotion. It can turn into a phobia when the anticipation, or anxiety is so great that it interferes with everyday life.

I will not let this happen. I will face my fears and evaluate them logically so that I can create a defense for each of my concerns that will put the power back in my hands.

Follow this process for yourself. Write down your fears no matter how silly you think they sound. Write them down and honor them. Then, think about a logical response to each fear and write that down as well. Use the power of your response to weaken the power of the fear.

You are stronger than you realize, and you can conquer fear and anxiety. You can do it. I promise.

Healing Inspiration:

Psalm 27: 14
Wait patiently for the Lord. Be brave and courageous. Yes, wait patiently for the Lord.

Journal Reflections:

1. How has your cancer journey challenged your ability to trust?

2. Write down what scares you most, then sit back, and evaluate it without emotion. How can you change your thought pattern so that this "monster" does not scare you so much?

CHAPTER 39

OMG, No Bucket List?

One thing that hit me very hard as I prepared for my fourteen-hour cancer surgery and the subsequent recovery was that I did not have a bucket list.

Oh my gosh. I had not prepared a "do it before I die" list. *How am I supposed to live this new life after-cancer with a renewed spirit if I don't even have a bucket list?*

A bucket list is supposed to be fun; a wish list of fun and adventure that brings new life to your soul.

But I did not have a bucket list. There was no wish list. This was terrible. I realized, yet again, that I had spent so much of my life achieving work goals and providing for others, that I forgot about ME.

The saying "Never get so busy making a living that you forget to make a life" comes to mind and seems appropriate for what my life has become. At this point, I wasn't even sure what I wanted my life to be. *Who am I? What makes my heart sing?*

It was time to make my list. It was time to stop letting busyness stop me from enjoying my life. This was another post-cancer lesson.

I am excited and a bit nervous. *Do I really get to pick all the things that make ME happy?* That is incredible. I have never thought that way before. It felt very liberating.

It is time to dream. It is time to fill my bucket list.

Healing Inspiration:

John 3: 3
Jesus answered and said to him, "Amen, amen, I say to you, no one can enter the kingdom of God without being born of water and Spirit.

Journal Reflections:

1. *Do you have a bucket list? If not, take time today to dream of adventures, trips, events, or accomplishments that would make you feel happy. Start your list.*

2. *Are you making time for yourself today? Carve out some quiet time and dream of the adventures you would have if time, money, and circumstance had no impact on your plans.*

CHAPTER 40

I am Lost

What I have found amazing throughout this cancer journey is how past life lessons are replaying in my head and in my dreams. It is like the universe is trying to teach me many important lessons.

I have had a recurring dream for a while now. It is the same dream each time - I am lost, I am rushing, and I can't find what I am looking for. I become more and more anxious as I search to find my way... but I cannot. I never get there. I am always lost. I am scared and lost.

Now, I think I understand.

I think I feel lost because I have not been true to who I am. Maybe I have been so busy fixing, climbing, achieving, and attaining, that I never took time for my emotional well-being. I never gave myself the freedom to dream about who I really wanted to be. I chose a career that made me a lot of money, but did it really make my heart happy? Was I living the life I was meant to live?

Now, I stand battered from a cancer fight with an extra emptiness in my heart. *Who am I? I do not want to be lost anymore. Where do I begin? What is my purpose?*

The meaning of life is an awful big subject and not one that can be solved in a few chapters. But for me, it started by answering a few questions:

1. What makes me smile?
2. What makes me feel great about myself?
3. What am I naturally good at?
4. What are my deepest values?

I want to take more time for myself, to feel more of my emotions and honor what they may be trying to teach me. I value meaningful relationships and want to connect with people on a deeper level. I want to give more than I take. I want to help when I can and get help when I need it.

I don't want to feel lost anymore.

Healing Inspiration:

Journal Reflections:

1. *Are you living your authentic life? If not, what changes can you make to draw closer to that person?*

2. *What is stopping you from making changes in your life? Trust your heart. You know the way; just trust it.*

CHAPTER 41

My Own Hotel California

After being diagnosed with cancer and successfully maneuvering through the urgent treatment plan, surgery, and recovery, I was left with a new kind of emptiness; the emptiness of "now what." *What am I supposed to do now? How do I move forward?*

In talking with many ladies who have gone before me on this crazy journey, I am told that the after-effects of cancer can last a long time. The physical healing is in some ways easier and shorter in duration than the mental and spiritual healing that seems to linger much longer.

It feels like my own version of Hotel California:

> "...and I was thinking to myself, this could be Heaven, or this could be Hell...." You can check out, but you can never leave."

It never leaves. It has been four months since my first surgery and almost one month since my second and today I am mad all over again.

Mad and very sad.

I don't want to deal with this anymore. I don't want to burst into tears because my scars are screaming, and I can't take another minute of the pain. I do not want to have a panic attack because I am suddenly having chest pain from the nerve damage of a double mastectomy. *I just want to be normal again. Please.*

But this is the new normal and I must find a way to cope. I must implement new strategies to combat these feelings of anger, sadness, and fear. I cannot always struggle with these same issues over and over again.

And then it dawned on me. Prayer is the strongest defense I know. *God, please help me through this. Please help me find my way.*

Each time the pain consumes me, or the panic attack begins to take hold, I stop myself, take slow deep breaths and begin to pray. I pray until the feelings subside. Sometimes I can barely focus on the words, but I keep going as focused as I can. It is a strong defense against pain and fear.

I know that one day I will look back at this time in my life and it won't hurt so much. I know that time will help heal this wound. By the grace of God, I will grow stronger and wiser than I am today.

"You can check out, but you can never leave."

That's OK, I don't need to leave. I am fine right here.

I am just fine.

Healing Inspiration:

Mark 11: 24
Therefore, I tell you, all that you ask for in prayer, believe that you will receive it and it shall be yours.

Journal Reflections:

1. *What is your biggest struggle today? Send an extra prayer to God that he may deliver strength for you to conquer your fears.*

2. *Plan something fun today. Get outside. Go to the movies. Laugh. This cancer journey is a heavy burden and the more you can offset it with joy and laughter, the weaker it becomes. Stay strong, dear warrior.*

Part Seven

Making Friends with the Enemy

CHAPTER 42

Deferment is Too Expensive

H ave you heard the saying "you can pay me now, or you can pay me later?" This saying seems very applicable right now.

If you do not identify and deal with emotions, both happy and sad, at the time they occur, often times these feelings will bury themselves in your subconscious to be used on another day. The feelings may come spilling out when you least expect it.

You know how it works - you are at a particular event and you have an extreme emotional reaction to something that seems trivial but for you raises great emotion. Has that happened to you?

For me, it was a wedding. It was a beautiful day and a happy event, but because of unresolved sadness I carried from an event in my past, the tears started to flow, and I just could not stop them. I had to excuse myself and regain my composure.

This is a result of emotional deferment. On that day, it was clear to me that I had not completely dealt with the feelings from my past and now they had bubbled up to the top and demanded my attention.

Cancer has a way of accelerating the boiling point.

This is another lesson I have learned. There is no way to get around the emotional impacts of cancer, the only way was to go through the process, one step at a time.

I encourage you to look for unresolved issues that reside within your heart. You know what they are. Write them down, think about them, forgive yourself and others, and then, let them go.

You can't move forward from the past until you completely addressed the unresolved issues. It can hurt, and most of the time we bury issues because they hurt too much at the time. But it doesn't get easier and sometimes the hurt gets stronger as time goes by. But now is the time to resolve your issues. All of them. It is for your own wellbeing.

You have just beaten the biggest monster of all and now you have superpowers to address these unresolved issues. Take advantage of these super-powers and dive in. Name the issues and then, let them go. Let them go forever and give yourself the space to create new happy memories.

There is great relief is resolving the past. it clears your vision for a brighter future.

You can do this, remember, your super-powers!

Healing Inspiration:

Colossians 3: 12-13
Put on then, as God's chosen ones, holy and beloved, heartfelt compassion, kindness, humility, gentleness and patience, bearing with one another and forgiving one another, If one has a grievance against another; as the Lord has forgiven you, so must you also do.

Journal Reflections:

1. What past hurts still live in your heart? Are you waiting for an apology that might never come? Let it go today. Release the tension of that hurt and allow yourself to move on.

2. Congratulations dear warrior: you are becoming stronger and stronger during this time of recovery. Be proud of yourself.

CHAPTER 43

Too Much Empathy

T he all-inclusive healing package for cancer seems to include three things: physical, mental, and spiritual healing. I feel like I have addressed the physical and mental healing, but now, I am left with the question of how to heal my soul? Where do I begin?

As I wander through my past and consciously acknowledge unresolved issues, I find a common theme. In most cases, I realize it is a matter of release. It's not really an unresolved issue as much as it just needs to be set free. *I am carrying way too much baggage.*

I have always been the strong one, the shoulder for everyone to lean on. People come to me to share their stories and what I realized through this cancer journey, is that often I internalized their problems and worked to find a solution as if it were my issue. I have learned that I have too much empathy.

Cancer was the straw that broke my camel's back. It taught me another important lesson. It is for my own good that I must rebalance this emotion. I must drop these heavy burdens and set myself free. I must learn that not everything is my issue to solve.

I can't be strong for everyone else. I can't own your issue or solve your problem. I can only muster enough strength to deal with my own issues. Don't get me wrong. In most cases, you didn't ask me to solve your problem, I usually just took on that role myself.

When others hurt - I hurt. When others suffer - I suffer. That is how it has been for as long as I can remember. And, what I have come to realize is that I have made it my mission to fix other people's problem - whatever it was, I fixed it. But I cannot do it anymore.

A dear friend explained it this way:

> "God brings each of us into this world with our own individual spiritual journey that includes a variety of challenges meant to help teach that person lessons of strength and encouragement along the way.
>
> If you intervene and carry someone else's burden, two things happen; 1) your bucket becomes overflowing with too many challenges and 2) you rob the other person of their own spiritual journey with God."

I never thought of it that way. I never thought that I was taking away from someone else's spiritual journey. I thought I was being helpful by easing their burden, but, it is not my burden and it is not my place to take it away from someone else.

I'm sorry if I overshadowed your personal journey. I didn't mean to take anything away from you.

From now on, I will be different. I will continue to be a good listener, but I won't fix other people's problems. I will be there for support and will try not to take too much control.

You must take care of yourself. It is for my own good.

Healing Inspiration:

Proverbs 19: 8
He who gains intelligence is his own best friend;
He who keeps understanding will be successful

Journal Reflections:

1. *Do you struggle with forgoing your own needs to satisfy the needs of others? What steps can you take to make your needs a top priority?*

2. *Are you traveling your own spiritual journey, or carrying the burdens of others? What can you do to change this thought pattern and release yourself from this obligation? We must all walk our own journey.*

CHAPTER 44

Forgiveness

As I continue to heal my mind and my spirit, the next big roadblock on my journey is forgiveness. It is textbook healing, right? One must forgive so that they can move on. That is absolutely right.

For me, it is about changing how I view my personal scorecard. I have always been a goal-oriented person with a black-and-white view of success – I either succeeded or I failed – it was that simple, there was no grey area.

Throughout my cancer journey, I have learned that the black-and-white scorecard is not a healthy way to view my life. It puts too much pressure on me and forces me past all the middle-ground where most of life's joy resides.

Forgiveness has been proven to lead to better health, lower heart rate, blood pressure and improved sleep. Forgiveness has been shown to restore positive thoughts, feelings, and behaviors.

As another lesson along my cancer journey, I have learned that I must forgive myself and others more often. By doing so, I will liberate myself from the thoughts of anger or revenge and find gratitude in what lies before me. I have been missing much of life's simple joy and it is time to change the lens and forgive myself and others for past transgressions.

I am moving on to a brighter place. I am moving to a place of joy.

Healing Inspiration:

John 3: 32
And you will know the truth, and the truth will set you free.

Journal Reflections:

1. *Describe a time when you forgave a loved one for something that hurt you? How did it feel for you when you released this hurt?*

2. *Forgiveness is the most freeing thing we can do for ourselves as we continue down this healing path. Write down 5 things you are still carrying with you from past hurts. Can you let them go today?*

CHAPTER 45

Trust

The textbook definition of trust is the belief that someone or something is reliable, good, honest, and effective.

But who can we trust? What is reliable?

This is an attribute that has been most damaged during my breast cancer journey. I don't trust anything anymore. I felt betrayed with all that I used to know. I trusted that healthy living would bring health. I always did the right thing, and I thought it would give me the right life. But it didn't turn out that way. It gave me cancer.

I feel totally betrayed. I followed all the rules and did all the right things and I got cancer. There must be some mistake.

But after working through the emotions of anger and fear, I now see that it is time for me to rebuild trust in my life. This brings me to one of the final steps in the grieving process - the step of acceptance.

Rebuilding trust takes time. It takes baby steps toward healing the betrayal. It takes letting go and forgiveness. It takes time.

I am learning to trust, not that I will have a perfect life or be without unexpected challenges, but that God has a plan for me.

I trust that He has a plan.

Healing Inspiration:

Jeremiah 28: 11-12
For I know well the plans I have in mind for you, says the Lord, plans for your welfare, not for woe? Plans to give you a future full of hope. When you look for me, you will find me.

Journal Reflections:

1. *How has your trust been shaken as a result of your cancer journey?*

2. *What can you do to strengthen your trust today?*

CHAPTER 46

The Healing Ritual of Fire

Today, I gathered all my troubles and burned them.

I learned about this awesome healing ritual from a dear friend of mine. He told me to write down everything that was still weighing heavy on my heart and then have my own little bonfire.

This is a simple, yet powerful ritual to release all the things that make you unhappy. *Boy, I am all for that. Let's give it a try.*

So, I take time to write down each thing that continues to weigh heavy on my heart; things that went wrong, hurts that have not healed, pain that is unresolved.

I wrote one item on each little slip of paper and I kept writing until I could not think of anymore items. Soon, I had my own little pile of kindling. I laughed at how many pieces of paper I had accumulated. *I guess I've been carrying more burdens than I realized.*

Now, the next step was to burn this lovely pile of burden! But, be safe so you do not burn your house down.

I have an outdoor firepit, so I gathered my pieces of paper and headed outside. I carefully read each item out load as I placed it into the fire pit where I had already prepared the kindling so when I threw the match, it would burn.

The release of emotions was very powerful even before I light the fire. Tears were welling up in my eyes by the time I reached for the final slip of paper. After carefully arranging my "troubles" over the kindling, I set the kindling on fire and watched everything burn.

I allowed the fire to burn out and then said a prayer to God.

Thank you for making me strong. Thank you for giving me life and for being patient with me as I move through my journey. Please watch over me and my family and guide our way. In Jesus' name, Amen.

Now, it is done, there is no going back. I can't put all those little pieces of paper back together to rebuild my burdens, so I have to let them go.

My troubles were now just a pile of ash. I am free of the emotional tether that these issues have had on me, and I am free to move forward. No more looking back. I feel strong and ready to move forward with new feelings of hope.

The fire has burned out and I am free to move forward.

Healing Inspiration:

1 Peter 1: 3-4

Blessed be the God and Father of our Lord Jesus Christ, who in his great mercy gave us anew birth to a living hope through the resurrection of Jesus Christ from the dead, to an inheritance that is imperishable, undefiled, and unfading, kept in heaven for you.

Journal Reflections:

1. *Did you have your own bonfire? How did it feel?*

2. *Think of ways that you can release heavy emotions each day; don't carry unresolved burdens; they are too heavy and should not be part of our healing journey.*

CHAPTER 47

But Now I am Found

I am feeling stronger each day as my body continues to heal. I feel confident that I can do more things today than I could a month ago. I am beginning to trust my body again.

I feel like I have transformed.

I am not lost anymore.

When I started my cancer journey, I knew there would be lessons that I was meant to learn. I knew this journey was going to be the hardest battle I had fought during my life so far.

I knew there were only two choices: be strong and get through this or don't. As cancer warriors, we only have those two choices – be strong and get through, or don't. There is no in-between.

Although when looking at the two choices, at least for me, there was only one answer. *I must be strong; I must do it.* The choice of giving up was not an option for me and understanding that I actually had a choice and that my choice was to be strong and get through this storm, helped me to feel like I had some control. I had made an intentional choice; to be strong and to fight cancer.

A dear friend told me a long time ago "you always have a choice, you just might not like the options, and it won't always be easy, but you will always have a choice. Always."

When I framed my cancer journey through this lens, I felt stronger. My choice was to be strong. It was MY choice, and not cancer's choice. I would do what had to be done.

I will survive and I will thrive!

Healing Inspiration:

Ezekiel 36: 26-27
I will give you a new heart and place a new spirit within you, taking from your bodies your stony hearts and giving you natural hearts. I will put my spirit within you.

Journal Reflections:

1. *How has your cancer journey changed the way you view your world?*

2. *Be still and listen to what your heart is telling you. Follow your heart, it knows the way.*

Part Eight

Cancer's Gifts

CHAPTER 48

Time for a Change

I used to read a lot of self-help books. I read books like The Secret and that said, "You are what you think", and it all sounded so simple. All anyone needed to do was to project your intentions to the universe and you would receive whatever you wished for. I read the book years ago and thought "ppshh, that a bunch of whooey".

But since everyone was raving about how awesome the technique was for manifesting good things in life, I decided to jump on the bandwagon and give it a try.

I thought hard about what I wanted, and I tried to be as clear as possible. What did I want from the world? I named my intention and thought hard about it for a few days and .... I got nothin'. Nothing ever came. Nothing ever changed, and it was just as I suspected. It was a bunch of whooey.

Despite my pessimism back then, I now felt compelled to give it another try. Things were different and maybe it would work this time. I knew that I needed to make some positive changes in my life, and for some reason, this technique kept presenting itself to me, so I decided to try again.

Maybe it was because I was more open to new ideas, or maybe it was because I had finally slowed down enough to be able to really hear myself think. But whatever it was, something definitely happened this time.

I figured it out. Throughout my whole life, whenever I had a problem that I couldn't solve or something that weighed very heavy on my mind, it would often sort itself out while I was sleeping. I would wake up with new ideas of ways to solve the issue and a very strong idea of what to do.

Last night, a big clue dropped into my dreams.

My mind was fixated on how hard my life had been. For years I focused on how hard things were, and I often recounted my accumulated hardships, like a scorecard. Things like multiple miscarriages, the struggle with trying to achieve work/life balance while flying around the globe 75k miles per year, divorce, and now, cancer. You get the idea. I was really good at having pity parties. Poor Me.

But now I think I get it. I need to stop keeping score. Life is always going to be hard, but so what? I need to stop keeping score of the things that have gone wrong in my life and start keeping track of everything that has gone right. I need to focus on the good things.

I need to think more about what I have done right instead of what I have done wrong. This is my AHA moment.

It is time to change. *I cannot let the rain cloud block the sun any longer. I must escape, and so today is a new day.* I am going to consciously create my new (positive) intentions and toss them into the universe.

I am sure it will work this time.

Healing Inspiration:

Philippians 4: 8-9
Finally, brothers, whatever is true, whatever is honorable, whatever is just, whatever is pure, whatever is lovely, whatever is gracious, if there is any excellence and if there is anything worthy of praise, think about these things. Keep on doing what you have learned and received and heard and seen in me. Then the God of peace will be with you.

Journal Reflections:

1. *Create a set of intentions for yourself and read them out loud each morning and each night. Say them with conviction and believe in them.*

2. *Look back on the progress you have made throughout your cancer journey. Congratulate yourself! You have come a long way, baby!*

CHAPTER 49

Alone Does Not Mean Lonely

Our society places too much pressure on single people. We have created an unhealthy definition of what it means to be alone. If you are alone... there must be something wrong with you.

This is completely wrong.

I know people who can't stand to be alone. It drives them crazy and they don't know what to do with the silence. They avoid being alone with themselves to whatever extreme necessary.

I, on the other hand, like to be alone. I have always enjoyed time by myself and that doesn't mean there is something wrong with me. I enjoy the peace and quiet and I enjoy disconnecting.

I think it should be mandatory for people to spend a certain amount of time alone. Alone time is necessary for you to be able to hear what is in your heart. Learning to be alone gives you time to become more self-aware so that you can discover who you really want to be. You cannot find your independence and true self if you are constantly surrounded by others.

I have always believed that God speaks to you in your heart. I think that often we know the right answer to our challenges, but with too much external influence, we are too afraid to trust our inner voice.

Throughout my cancer journey I have had a lot of time to myself and I have had time to clear away much of the noise and nonsense that I filled my life with. I am thankful for this time because it has given me a newfound love for ME.

As much as I thought I was in control of my own destiny, the lesson of cancer gave me a new perspective. *I am not as afraid as I used to be. I have let go of many of the trivial worries of my past and I am ok.* I am much more self-confident because I got myself through this crazy storm.

I am strong. I am a warrior and I am going to be ok.

Be strong and step into your own light. Trust yourself.

You know the way. You can do this!

Healing Inspiration:

Proverbs 3: 5-6
Trust in the Lord with all your heart,
on your own intelligence rely not;
in all your ways be mindful of him,
and he will make straight your paths.

Journal Reflections:

1. *Do you spend time alone? How does it make you feel?*

2. *What problems are you struggling with today? Ask God for guidance in solving these problems.*

CHAPTER 50

Letting Go

There is real value in being appreciated.

We all want to be needed by others. We want people close to us to acknowledge our needs and feelings just as much as we acknowledge theirs. We want to feel like we matter and that we make a difference.

But sometimes the need to be appreciated causes an unhealthy imbalance. Sometimes we end up giving too much of ourselves away, and sometimes what we are holding on to is toxic for us.

It may be time to let go.

I have learned that it is time for me to let go, and I can tell you that it sure feels awesome.

Why are we so afraid to let go? Maybe we are afraid that we will not be needed and thereby we will no longer be valuable. Or maybe we are afraid to take a chance, or that we might look silly, or a million other reasons.

This has been one of my biggest lessons, and I can tell you this for sure - once you learn to let go of what no longer serves you, you will see that it becomes easier each time you are challenged in the future. I think of it visually, as in physically letting go of a swinging trapeze bar.

Try it. Start small. Pick a problem or a worry that you are ready to give up. Make it worthwhile but don't pick your biggest one. For now, start small.

Now, visualize yourself letting go of that worry in the same way you would let go of a trapeze bar. Take time to really visualize the process.

Let it go.

If you keep struggling to grab ahold again, stop yourself. For now, make this worry "finished." You cannot grab ahold because that bar is already gone. Think of it as being a trapeze artist. You cannot grab the next bar that is coming toward you until you completely let go of the bar you were holding on to before. For a split second, you are holding on to nothing.

This is it. This is where you are free.

Now grab hold of the new bar and visualize that old worry as leaving with the bar that is now swinging behind you. There is no going back.

This is how it starts; one worry at a time. Let go of the bar. Grab what is in front of you and keep going.

Trust me.

Healing Inspiration:

Philippians 4: 6-7
Have no anxiety at all, but in everything, by prayer and petition, with thanksgiving, make your requests known to God. Then the peace of God that surpasses all understanding will guard your hearts and minds in Christ Jesus.

Journal Reflections:

1. *How do you handle "letting go"? Is it easy or hard for you? Why?*

2. *Make today a "worry free" day. Set all worries aside and just enjoy the beauty of the day. You deserve it. Enjoy your day!*

CHAPTER 51

Faith is the Beginning

I have learned to let go and now I am learning to have faith.

I was born and raised Catholic, so faith is not a new concept to me. But I did not fully understand what it meant until I was diagnosed with cancer. Cancer taught me in a matter of months what a lifetime of Catholic faith could not.

I thought, if I had both control and faith, that it would give me an added boost - it was a hedge in case one or the other wasn't working. I always had a back-up plan. If faith didn't work – I would have control to fall back on. I could take the reins and fix whatever was going wrong. I would let God try first and then if it didn't go my way, I would take the reins and try to control the situation (or at least that's was I thought).

Nope. It does not work that way. Having control is an illusion and faith is all there is.

After enduring eight months of pain on my own personal cancer journey, I have long abandoned the illusion of control, and I have learned that instead, I must have faith.

Faith that things are as they should be. Faith that I will find the strength and courage to deal with what is presented to me.

Faith is not an act, it is an attitude, an understanding that things will work out as they should.

I am still learning, but today, I choose to have an attitude of faith.

Healing Inspiration:

Hebrews 11: 6
But without faith it is impossible to please him, for anyone who approaches God must believe that he exists and that he rewards those who seek him.

Journal Reflections:

1. *How is your faith? Do you believe that things are as they should be?*

2. *What can you do today to strengthen your faith? Can you hear Jesus calling?*

CHAPTER 52

Riding the Lazy River

I t seems to me that life is a bit like an amusement park.

There are choices we make about the level of excitement we decide to participate in. Are you a wild daredevil or a calm easy stroll through the park?

Me? I am a strong Type A and I am going all-in. Go big or go home. I will always head toward the roller coaster and the biggest scariest rides in the amusement park. My friend, who is a Steady-Eddie Type B, is much more interested in the Ferris wheel, merry-go-round, or lazy river.

I have always thought life was Black-or-White. Win-or-Lose. Right-or-Wrong, My-Way-or-The Highway. I always ignored the middle ground, because I thought it was just noise and that it was a distraction that slowed me down from getting the real prize.

I never realized until today that there are many other options. Today I finally realized that my Win-or-Lose, Right-or-Wrong mentality is the flaw in my thinking. I think I understand, and I have learned another lesson on my cancer journey. *The grey area is not so bad after all.*

I have realized that I can be at the amusement park and not always ride the roller coaster. I can choose to ride the Ferris wheel or float down the lazy river. It still makes my trip to the amusement park a wonderful experience. I can relax and enjoy the calm. I do not always need to be full throttle. Itis OK to dial-it-down.

Today, I am riding the lazy river and it's awesome!

Healing Inspiration:

1 Timothy 6: 6-7
Now there is great gain in godliness with contentment. For we brought nothing into the world, just as we shall not be able to take anything out of it.

Journal Reflections:

1. *Do you struggle with always have to achieve more and have more?*

2. *Lean back today. Practice the art of contentment and see how relaxed it makes you feel.*

CHAPTER 53

A Hint of Joy

My grandson spent the day with me. He is eighteen months old and knows exactly what he wants. It reminded me that once, a long time ago, I knew exactly what I wanted too. Then, life got busy and time slipped away, and I forgot about the things that brought me joy.

As cliché as it sounds, it is true - it is the simple things that mean the most. *Yeah, yeah. We all know that, and it sounds nice, like rainbows and unicorns, but come on, life is hard and simple things don't always fix it, right?*

But, they can. Simple things can fix it all.

No matter how stressed your day or how difficult your life, if you set it all aside, I mean really set it aside, you will find an opening in your heart that can show you a hint of joy, even if it's just for a few minutes.

I remember when my girls were little, and I would go to one of their games, either soccer or basketball. Once I was able to settle in, shut my phone off and really engage in the activities, it felt so good. There was such joy in these events, as simple as they were, they were often the best part of my day.

If you are paying attention and your heart is open, you will find it too, a hint of joy. Cherish it, repeat it as often as possible and soon, what you thought was hard yesterday might not seem quite as hard today.

Give yourself a break. Find your joy.

Healing Inspiration:

James 1: 2-4
Consider it all joy, my brothers, when you encounter various trials, for you know that the testing of your faith produces perseverance. And let perseverance be perfect, so that you may be perfect and complete, lacking in nothing.

Journal Reflections:

1. *List five things that bring you joy. Are these things part of your everyday life?*

2. *What can you do to remember to find joy every day?*

CHAPTER 54

Am I an Instrument?

I have not picked up my Bible in years, but today I felt a strong urge to find it. I didn't know why, but I knew I needed to find it. It was packed in a box in the garage somewhere, but there were so many to pick from, where was my Bible?

After much searching, I found it. Yippee! I felt happy and relieved.

But, now what? I wasn't sure what I was looking for. I held the Bible in my hand. *Where do I begin?* There were some 1800 pages in the Bible and how in the world would I know where to start? I had not looked at it in years and I wasn't sure what had compelled me to find it today.

As I flipped through the pages, I found in the center of the Bible that there were prepared study lessons for a variety of life situations. I paged through to see what sounded interesting.

There is was. Lesson #57 - Picking Up the Pieces. That one jumped out at me and it felt right.

I read the summary and tears welled up in my eyes after a few short paragraphs "Do you feel lost? Are you alone with your anger? Are you ready to heal your wounds?" *Yes, this is where I will begin.*

The study guide confirmed many of the lessons that I had already throughout my cancer journey:

- Forgiveness
- Gratitude
- Trust in Self
- Trust in God

The scripture readings showed examples of how to ask God for strength, show kindness to others and expect nothing in return.

Before today, I had been afraid to ask for God's help. I felt like maybe he was mad at me and was punishing me for my sins. I thought if I asked for help, he might turn up the heat. I felt punishable but I didn't really know why. But I knew I wanted to stay off the radar for future wrath. It was a little like if God didn't notice me, maybe he wouldn't pick me for that next hardship. *I am not strong enough for another hardship.*

However, I learned through reading this particular lesson, that God does not distribute wrath, he forgives us for our sins and does not send punishment. *These are the exact words I needed to hear today.*

After much self-reflection, I was still struggling with why I got cancer. I still felt let down and betrayed. I had always tried to do the right thing and had sacrificed my needs for the needs of others, yet I was the one who got cancer.

Then it came. I turned the page and found The Prayer of St Francis.

Lord, make me an instrument of your peace.

Where there is hatred, let me sow love; where there is injury, pardon; where there is doubt, faith; where there is despair, hope; where there is darkness, light; where there is sadness, joy.

O, Divine Master, grant that I may not so much seek to be consoled as to console; to be understood as to understand; to be loved as to love; For it is in giving that we receive; it is in pardoning that we are pardoned; it is in dying that we are born again to eternal life.

This was like a lightning bolt for me.

Was I being asked to be an instrument? Was I being asked to show others the possibility of their own strength?

Many people have told me that I am the strongest person they know. And that if anyone could handle a hard situation, it was me. Maybe God is asking me to share this gift with others. Could it be he wanted me to be an instrument; to show others the possibility of their own strength? There is always a way home.

For it is in giving that we receive; it is in pardoning that we are pardoned; it is in dying that we are born again to eternal life.

Maybe that is why I have endured this terrible storm. Maybe God wanted my help.

Ok. I will try. I will try to reach out to others and try to help them understand that they are stronger than they think.

I will try to give to others without sacrificing my needs. I have learned that my needs must come first, but that I also have the strength to share with others.

Lord, make me an instrument of your peace.

Healing Inspiration:

Luke 6: 38
Give and gifts will be given to you; a good measure, packed together, shaken down and overflowing, will be poured into your lap. For the measure with which you measure will in return be measured out to you.

Journal Reflections:

1. *What gifts can you share with others?*

2. *Reach out to someone you think could use a helping hand today. Give what they need and be a blessing in their day.*

CHAPTER 55

By the Grace of God

My cancer journey has been one of deep reflection and self-awakening.

Without the forced time-out, I would likely have continued my life at a feverish pace with too many commitments and not enough hours in the day to accomplish them. Go. Go. More. More. More.

I feel like I owe cancer a big Thank You.

Thank you for this forced journey and thank you for the lessons I have learned.

We are all intensely aware of the things that cancer takes from us, but we do not often acknowledge the gifts it leaves behind. We hear of the bad, the sad and the painful, but we do not hear enough of the rebirth, the readjustment, and the reawakening.

It is by the grace of God that I have this new chance.

I knew from the day I was diagnosed, that cancer would demand my complete and undivided attention. It demanded that I stop and deal with what I could not control, and what I needed to heal - both emotionally and spiritually. My physical healing would happen alongside these other important lessons.

I was forced to shine a light on the deep dark shadows of my heart, heal wounds and learn lessons.

I feel more complete than when I began this journey.

Thank you, cancer.

Healing Inspiration:

Psalm 107: 28-29
In their distress they cried to the Lord,
who brought them out of their peril,
hushed the storm to a murmur;
the waves of the sea were stilled.

Journal Reflections:

1. *Is there a lesson that cancer taught you for which you are now thankful? Describe it.*

2. *Congratulations, dear warrior. The storm is subsiding and the sun is shining through. Celebrate your progress!*

CHAPTER 56

I Love ME

Today I am going to try something new - I am going to treat myself like I would treat my best friend. I will be thoughtful and kind to ME.

Here is another idea. Identify two or three things that would make your heart happy today. Name them, but don't overthink it or rationalize your choices. Just name them.

Now, go and find a way to do them.

If you have a million reasons why you can't - just stop. Try something new today, just for one day and then tomorrow, you can go back to your old ways if you want. Call in sick. Get a babysitter for the kids. Clear your calendar.

You would do these things for your best friend and now you need to do them for yourself. YOU are your best friend today.

Being your own best friend can be a great way to work through feelings of loneliness, insecurity, and instability in your life. God knows that walking through this cancer journey is lonely, insecure, and unstable, so what better gift to give yourself than the gift of friendship.

Throw caution to the wind and give it a try, be your own best friend.

Healing Inspiration:

1 Peter 5: 10-11
The God of all grace who called you to his eternal glory through Christ Jesus will himself restore, confirm, strengthen, and establish you after you have suffered a little. To him be dominion forever. Amen.

Journal Reflections:

1. *What makes your heart happy?*

2. *What did you do for yourself today to be your own best friend?*

CHAPTER 57

Dare to Do Great Things

Today I feel stronger. I may slip back into old patterns now and again, but overall, I feel stronger. I want to embrace this new strength and view life through my post-cancer lens so that I don't take things for granted.

I want to live more spontaneously and have more adventures. What do I have to lose?

The final and most important lesson I have learned through my cancer journey is do not wait.

Do not procrastinate your dreams; find what makes your soul happy and find a way to do more of it each and every day.

Do not regret your past, it has been the path that brought you to where you are today. You could not have arrived at this destination without having first made stops at the other parts of your past – the good, the bad and the ugly. It is all part of the journey. Now, embrace the future.

Do not be afraid. Trust yourself and have a little faith. Like my Mom used to always tell me, "Life is what you make it", so make it good. Let go of what you cannot control.

Love yourself and dare to do great things.

Healing Inspiration:

Journal Reflections:

1. *What do you aspire to be? What "great thing" is part of your spiritual journey?*

2. *Take steps today to strengthen your courage and make a plan to "do great things". You are a strong warrior, offer your strength to God and be an example to others.*

CHAPTER 58

A Big High-Five from Heaven

D o you ever see recurring numbers? For me, I see 11:11. Some days it is twice a day. I am not a clock-watcher and I can be busy working and quickly glance to see the time and wham.... It is 11:11 (again).

It used to freak me out, as if it were a premonition that something bad was about to happen. However, after a little research, I understand it is not a scary thing - it is a gift. It is the universe telling me to trust my heart.

It is the universe telling me everything is ok.

These sightings don't come all the time. They most often occur when I am in the midst of a big life-changing event. For the past several days I have seen 11:11 at least once, sometimes twice per day.

While visiting my Dad's gravesite recently, from nowhere came two dragonflies that gently hovered above while I stood and talked to my Dad. I noticed them and made the comment to others that dragonflies were good luck.

I felt like my Dad and my other angels in heaven were trying to give me a hug; a sign of encouragement and love that I was on the right path and that they were proud of me. I will take it. Thank you.

My dear cancer warrior, you are strong, and you are loved.

Believe in yourself and trust your heart.

Healing Inspiration:

Psalm 91: 11-12
For God commands the angels
to guard you in all your ways.
With their hands they shall support you,
lest you strike your foot against a stone.

Journal Reflections:

1. *How are your angels supporting you today?*

2. *Find a quiet place and meditate on the gifts that cancer has given you. You are a stronger person than when you began this journey. Celebrate your success. You are a Beautiful Lady.*

EPILOGUE

This has been quite a journey. Although forced and not what I would have chosen, it has been a rollercoaster of emotion and a spiritual transformation.

Cancer touches thousands of people each year and it leaves you a different person. Aside from the obvious physical changes, it also changes you emotionally, and spiritually.

I hope that my journey has given you strength that you can get through this and courage to work through your battles with the knowledge that it won't always be this hard and that there are often times hidden gifts along the way.

Keep your heart open, ask for the love and support of others, and trust yourself. You have all the courage you need to pull yourself through this darkness. You do. Trust yourself.

Reach out to your medical doctors. Ask for help with whatever you need; be it physical, mental, or spiritual. Do not be afraid to ask for help. There is such wonderful support from the breast cancer community, so take advantage of their services.

Most of all - breathe. Just breathe. Take one baby step at a time and soon you will see that the rays of sunshine are shining through your window again and you will begin to see your own hint of joy. Grab a hold of it and don't let it go. Embrace today and find what makes your heart sing. Sing loud and sing proud.

You deserve it. You fought the fight and you WON.

You have slayed the cancer monster and now you have the inner strength to conquer anything. You have earned your warrior badge. We all have. We have fought a tough fight and we WON. Congratulations, my fellow warriors.

Jesus replied, "My light will shine for you just a little longer.

Walk in the light while you can, so the darkness will not overtake you.

Those who walk in the darkness cannot see where they are going."

-John 12: 35

Let cancer be your catalyst and use it as a springboard for change. Write your own story. I promise, if you have the courage to shine the light on the dark places in your heart, you will see that God will give you the strength to heal. He will help you heal your mind, body and soul. Be the warrior you were born to be!

May God bring you peace and happiness.

The End